Cambridge English Readers
···
Level 5

Series editor: Philip Prowse

In the Shadow of the Mountain

Helen Naylor

T0382998

CAMBRIDGE
UNIVERSITY PRESS

CAMBRIDGE
UNIVERSITY PRESS

University Printing House, Cambridge CB2 8BS, United Kingdom

One Liberty Plaza, 20th Floor, New York, NY 10006, USA

477 Williamstown Road, Port Melbourne, VIC 3207, Australia

314–321, 3rd Floor, Plot 3, Splendor Forum, Jasola District Centre, New Delhi – 110025, India

79 Anson Road, #06–04/06, Singapore 079906

Cambridge University Press is part of the University of Cambridge.

It furthers the University's mission by disseminating knowledge in the pursuit of education, learning and research at the highest international levels of excellence.

www.cambridge.org
Information on this title: www.cambridge.org/9780521775519

© Cambridge University Press 1999

First published 1999

Printed in Great Britain by Ashford Colour Press Ltd.

A catalogue record for this publication is available from the British Library

ISBN 978-0-521-77551-9 Paperback

Contents

Chapter 1	Family lunch	6
Chapter 2	Telling Kevin	10
Chapter 3	Memory	12
Chapter 4	A chance to catch up	15
Chapter 5	Two letters	19
Chapter 6	Arriving in Zermatt	24
Chapter 7	The first steps	28
Chapter 8	Ulrich Grunwalder	31
Chapter 9	Ulrich's early life	35
Chapter 10	Edward Crowe	39
Chapter 11	Andrew calls	45
Chapter 12	Past and present	49
Chapter 13	A night out	54
Chapter 14	Information	57
Chapter 15	With Bruno's help	62
Chapter 16	Bruno's story	67
Chapter 17	Love story	70
Chapter 18	Shared experience	79
Chapter 19	The summer place	84
Chapter 20	The news breaks	90
Chapter 21	Burying Edward	94

Characters

Clare Newton: forty-six years old, divorced. A journalist. Lives in London.

Andrew Newton: younger brother of Clare. Married to Jan.

Marjorie Newton: in her late seventies; mother of Clare and Andrew. Married to Thomas Newton, who died a year before the story begins.

Edward Crowe: grandfather of Clare and Andrew; father of Marjorie. Married to Agatha.

Bruno: in his early forties; ski instructor and mountain guide in Zermatt.

Ulrich Grunwalder: ninety-four-year-old mountain guide, lives in Zermatt.

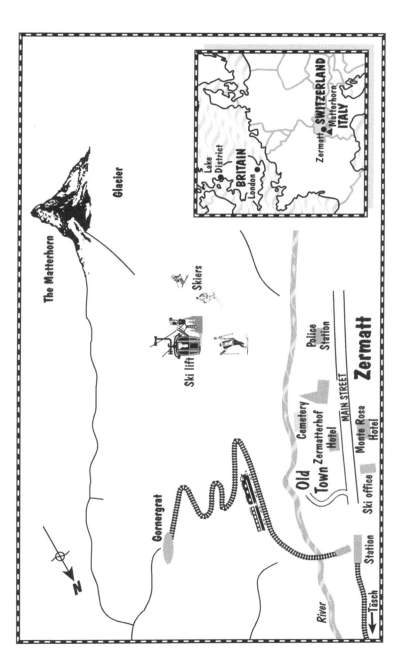

Chapter 1 *Family lunch*

On 23 April 1998, Edward Crowe came out from the glacier on the north side of the Matterhorn mountain above Zermatt in Switzerland. He had been dead for seventy-four years.

And on the same day, over 2,000 kilometres away, the three direct descendants of Edward Crowe – his daughter Marjorie and his two grandchildren, Clare and Andrew – were enjoying a rare day together at the family home in Windermere, centre of England's Lake District.

Clare had driven up from London the night before, arriving very late at her mother's house. She had slept deeply in her old childhood bed and hadn't woken until after nine o'clock. She'd stayed in bed for a few minutes, enjoying the quiet outside her window. Here, she was Clare the daughter again, rather than Clare the independent, successful journalist.

She loved coming home to Windermere, even though she'd had her own home and her own life down in London for many years. There was something about the northern part of England, and especially the Lake District where she'd grown up, that was part of her. Despite the awful 400 kilometre-plus journey up the M6 motorway ('Britain's biggest car park' someone had described it as), she always found herself relaxing the further north she got. Usually, by the time she turned off the motorway, it was dark and she couldn't see the rocky hills or the waters of Lake Windermere, but she knew they were there.

On this visit she was hoping that being back in this magical landscape would give her time to think about her future. She knew she couldn't continue working at the newspaper for much longer. It was not what she wanted any more. But giving it up was a frightening thought – what else was there in her life?

Now here she was, a forty-six-year-old woman sitting at the dining table with Andrew, the two of them enjoying their mother's cooking.

'Mum, you haven't lost your touch,' said Clare. 'This salmon's great. No-one makes it quite like you.'

'I don't know what's special about it,' replied her mother. 'It's only a bit of grilled salmon. I've been doing it the same way all these years.'

'Exactly,' said Clare. 'That's the whole point – it's very comforting to find that some things don't change.'

'Finish off this last piece then, one of you. I don't want any left,' said Marjorie with a smile.

'Thanks,' said Andrew. 'I'll have it. I'm sorry Jan and the kids couldn't come today. You know how it is, Saturdays are the only time they get to do all their sport and things, and Jan likes to be there for them.'

'I'm not going to be here for ever you know. I want to enjoy my grandchildren while I can,' said Marjorie, busying herself round the table.

'That's exactly what Grandma Agatha used to say about us, but, Mum, that's the first time I've heard you talk about . . .' said Andrew.

'Dying,' said Marjorie, finishing her younger child's sentence.

'There's nothing wrong, is there?' asked Clare anxiously.

'Nothing, apart from old age, as far as I know,' replied Marjorie. 'Anyway, don't pay any attention to me.'

'How's the garden, Mum?' asked Andrew. He felt somehow responsible for the way this conversation was going and he thought it better to re-direct it onto safer ground – although Marjorie's garden could hardly be described as safe ground. For as long as they could remember their mother had fought to make the garden do what she wanted, but it always seemed to have a way of biting back. Some years it was the weather that killed off all the flowers, other years some kind of evil disease seemed to take over and, almost overnight, eat all the young plants she'd just put in. It was a long-running story that was part of their shared family history.

'Well, thank you for asking, Andrew. I know this may surprise you both but I think I'm winning this year. Everything seems to be doing rather well,' said Marjorie, looking pleased. 'Your father would be proud of me.'

There was a silence around the table as they each remembered the person who had brought them together today. Thomas Newton had died a year ago. He'd been cutting the grass in front of the house when Marjorie found him.

'A heart attack,' the doctor had said. His death had left a big hole in all their lives.

'To Dad,' said Andrew, raising his glass; Clare and Marjorie echoed his words in quiet voices.

It was then that the telephone rang.

'I'll go,' said Clare, wiping away a few tears.

They could hear her talking in the hall, but when she came back in she looked shocked.

'That was the Foreign Office, Mum.'

'Good Lord,' said Andrew. 'What did they want?'

Marjorie looked at Clare with surprise and a little fear in her eyes.

'It's about your father, Edward. Apparently,' Clare continued, 'they've found his body. It's about to be recovered from the foot of a glacier in Zermatt and they want someone to go over there.'

Chapter 2 *Telling Kevin*

When they were children, Clare and Andrew had been proud of the fact that their grandfather had died while climbing a famous mountain in Switzerland. It gave a bit of excitement, a bit of mystery, to their family that none of their friends could match. Clare had even been on a skiing holiday to Zermatt when she was in her twenties, and had stood at the foot of the Matterhorn and marvelled at the thought of her grandfather still up there, frozen in the ice.

After lunch Clare took her mobile phone into the garden to ring her editor at the *Daily News*.

'What's my schedule like for the next ten days or so, Kevin?' Clare asked.

'You probably know that better than I do – why are you asking?' Kevin replied.

This'll make him jump, thought Clare as she said, 'I've got to go to Switzerland to pick up a body, and . . .'

'You what?' said Kevin. 'Whose body . . . what are you talking about?'

'You know I'm up at my mother's this weekend, well the Foreign Office rang at lunchtime today and announced, out of the blue, that my Grandpa Edward was just about to appear out of the bottom of a glacier in Zermatt and would someone from the family go and collect him.' Clare couldn't resist making the whole thing sound rather light-hearted. She sometimes enjoyed trying to shock her unimaginative editor.

'You make it sound as if you're going to pick something up from a Lost Property Office,' said Kevin, surprised.

Clare gave him the details of her grandfather's climbing accident in 1924, as far as she knew them. And then she asked to be away from the office for the next week or so.

'This could make a great piece for the paper. It's not exactly something that happens every day, is it? And there'd be the added interest of the article being written by the granddaughter,' said Kevin.

'No way. You're not going to get my family history for everyone to read,' replied Clare firmly.

'Nonsense,' Kevin said. 'It fits with the sort of things you've been doing recently – the human interest stories. It'll be a great read.'

Clare changed the subject. They talked about who would replace her over the next week or so. She was concerned about the interview she'd only just managed to set up with Cherry Gaskell, the ex-wife of England's latest football star. Although she wasn't particularly proud of the kind of journalism she'd been doing in recent months, she didn't really want anyone else to do this particular interview. It was going to be a big story and she wanted the credit for it.

'She'll probably cancel the whole thing if we send someone else to do the interview,' said Clare. 'I'll ring her and suggest another date.'

'OK, OK,' said Kevin. 'Do what you want. But let me know if there are any problems – I don't want to lose that story. And ring me when you've found out more about your Grandfather's reappearance too.'

Chapter 3 *Memory*

Marjorie went about the house in her usual way that afternoon. She was almost used to living alone now and was beginning to find it normal not to have to consider another person's needs. She missed Thomas, naturally – they'd been together for forty-seven years. It was the silence in the house that had been the strangest at first – the absence of another person's presence. The sounds that you don't realise are there, until they're not. Over the last year she had started listening to the radio to fill the space.

But now, as she moved about the kitchen, she could hear her children talking together in the living room and she enjoyed the sounds of life that they'd brought back into the house. She knew they'd be talking about their grandfather. It was quite extraordinary that the news of his reappearance should come today of all days.

But to be honest it wasn't news to Marjorie. She'd had a letter from the authorities about her father six months ago, but she hadn't told anyone. She'd put it to the back of her mind. Now it was here again – and it was going to be talked about, and she suddenly felt tired at the thought of it all. There would be all the questions and the paperwork to be faced, not to mention the funeral arrangements. She was glad that she could depend on Clare to sort it all out. Thank goodness for her efficient daughter. She'd always been a good organiser, since childhood, and Marjorie smiled as she remembered Clare at the age of five ordering all her toys in rows according to their size.

'Shall I make us all a cup of tea, Mum?' Clare asked.

'Yes please, dear,' said Marjorie. 'I think there's some cake in the blue tin, too.'

'OK,' said Clare. 'You go and sit down. I'll bring it in.'

Marjorie went through to the living room to join Andrew. 'How do you feel, Mum, about all this business with your father?' asked Andrew. 'It must be a bit of a shock.'

'Not really that much, dear,' replied his mother.

'Did you actually know about this before, Mum?' asked Clare coming in with the tea. 'The man on the phone said something – I can't remember what exactly – that made me think Grandfather had been expected.'

'That's right.' And Marjorie explained about the letter she'd received in November. 'I know it probably sounds strange, but I'd completely forgotten about it. You know what my memory's like at the moment.'

Clare knew exactly what her mother's memory was like; she also knew that this was not something she would have forgotten. More likely it was something she didn't want to think about.

'It seems an odd thing to forget,' said Andrew, echoing Clare's thoughts. 'But anyway, how do you feel about it?' he continued.

'I don't really know. After all, I was only four when he died so he wasn't a real part of my life. My mother, of course, never let me forget what a wonderful person he was, and how tragic his death was,' replied Marjorie with a small smile.

'Do you have any of your own memories of him at all?' asked Clare.

'No, sadly, I don't. Only what my mother told me.'

Marjorie reached forward to pick up her tea. Her hand shook slightly as she put the cup to her lips. Clare looked at her fondly and saw that her mother's eyes were full of tears.

Chapter 4 *A chance to catch up*

'I've just rung Jan and told her I'm staying here tonight,' said Andrew walking into the kitchen where Clare and his mother were chatting. Both women looked at him in surprise.

'Weren't you supposed to be taking her out for dinner tonight?' asked Marjorie.

'Yes, but I explained what had happened here, and we can go out another night,' replied Andrew, rather sharply. 'I know you both think Jan is the boss, but I am able to make my own decisions, you know.'

'Well, if you're sure, dear,' said Marjorie. 'I don't want you to get into trouble at home.'

'Mum, I'm not a child!' said Andrew angrily. 'I'm not going to get into trouble, as you call it. Jan is a perfectly reasonable woman. Anyway, I'm staying tonight, if that's all right. I thought you might be pleased,' said Andrew rather coolly.

'Of course I am. It's lovely to have you both here. Don't listen to me.'

Clare, who had remained silent during this part of the conversation, said, 'Well, in that case, Andrew, why don't you and I go to the pub for a quick drink. And we can pick up some takeaway pizzas on the way back. You'd be happy with a pizza tonight, wouldn't you Mum?'

'Lovely,' replied Marjorie. 'That'll give me time to have a

nice warm bath. And when you get back, there's something I want to show you both.'

*　　*　　*

Clare and Andrew sat together in the Lakeland Arms drinking the local beer and talking easily about the day and its events. In their childhood home, with all its memories and long-established patterns they found themselves slipping into the roles that had been set when they were young – Clare the bossy leader, and Andrew the quieter, indecisive one who was easily led. Here in the pub it was easier to talk as two normal adults who happened to be related.

Clare listened as Andrew talked about Jan and the kids, and seeing his face light up with pleasure as he told her of their latest adventures, she felt sad that she didn't see them more often. The fact that she and her ex-husband David had never had children hadn't worried her at the time. Actually, she'd been glad, especially when the marriage broke up after ten years. She knew she couldn't have managed with kids and working for the paper. But now, as she listened to Andrew, she felt something like jealousy. He had someone to care for and worry about, he had a clear path to the future. What did she have? No family certainly, only a job that she'd put all her energies into and which no longer satisfied her.

'Anyway,' said Andrew. 'Enough about my small world, what about you? I read your article about that lottery winner last week. A bit hard-hitting I thought. You certainly found some dirt on him.'

'Yes, well he deserved it,' replied Clare. 'He was so

unpleasant. Anyway, I thought it was quite good – it certainly caused a lot of reaction from readers.'

'Isn't he thinking about leaving the country now, after your article?' asked Andrew.

'So they say. The power of the press, you know.'

'Exactly,' replied Andrew, whose opinion of journalists was pretty low, even though his sister was one. He'd noticed that some of her recent articles and interviews had been getting more personal and he didn't like them. He preferred her work when she had studied her subjects in some depth and where she showed her strength as a writer and not as a journalist. He wondered whether he should tell her, but decided she was intelligent enough to have worked it out for herself. So he decided on a less direct approach.

'You seem to be writing different sorts of articles recently. Is this your choice or what?'

'It's all part of the public's never-ending desire for human interest stories,' said Clare rather bitterly. 'We have to write what sells papers. It's not something I'm particularly happy about, but that's how it is.'

In fact, Clare was very unhappy about the direction her work was taking. That was the problem; ever since the paper had been taken over by an American businessman, it had gone downmarket. And that was not just her opinion. Hundreds of newspaper articles had been written in other papers and magazines about the changes at the *Daily News*. In one article, by a man she'd always believed was a friend, her name had even been mentioned as someone who was helping to lower the standards. At first she'd been angry, because his words had hurt. But she knew he was right.

Andrew came back with another couple of drinks and said, 'Listen, do you want me to come with you to Zermatt to get grandfather?'

'No, there's no need. I can't imagine there'll be any problems. In any case, I think Mum is more upset by all this than she's saying. So it'll be good to have you here, in case,' said Clare.

She didn't tell him that she was glad to be going to Zermatt. Collecting Grandfather seemed like a good way of escaping from her empty life – if only for a short time.

'What do you think Mum wants to show us?' said Andrew.

'Maybe there's some dark secret about Grandfather that we don't know about,' laughed Clare.

'Well if there is, you'll certainly want to know all about it,' said Andrew. 'You never could stand a mystery, could you?'

'True,' said Clare. 'Anyway, let's get those pizzas and go back home. It's probably nothing to do with Grandfather.'

Chapter 5 *Two letters*

'I think you should read these, both of you,' said Marjorie handing over a couple of envelopes to Clare. 'The top one first.'

The envelopes were addressed to Mrs Agatha Crowe and had Swiss stamps on. Andrew sat on the arm of Clare's chair and they began reading:

May 11th, 1924
Zermatt
Dear Agatha

It is with great difficulty that I write this letter to you. You have every reason to be very angry.

I know that I have behaved badly towards you and little Marjorie. Believe me, it was not easy to leave you both.

I want you to know that I have made arrangements with Mr Tribble, the manager of Carfax Bank, Windermere for a bank account to be opened in your name into which I have placed a large amount of money. Regular monthly payments will be made so that you and Marjorie will be well-provided for.

My father, who has always had the highest regard for you, wishes to keep up his family duties, and to be a grandfather to Marjorie. I hope you will allow him to do so.

Yours
Edward

'Bloody hell, Mum. You mean he left her!' said Clare. 'Did she ever talk about it?'

'No,' said Marjorie quietly. 'Read the second one.'

June 12th, 1924
Zermatt
Dear Agatha

You know why I came here and you must understand that I am not going to return.

My father tells me that you have stopped him from visiting Marjorie and this hurts me. I believe that was your intention. I hope in the future you will find it in your heart to change your mind.

I shall not write again. It may be better for you and Marjorie to think of me as dead.

Yours
Edward

Clare and Andrew both looked shocked as they finished reading.

'And then, how long after that was he killed, Mum?' asked Andrew.

'About two months, on August 16th,' said Marjorie.

'Or was he? Maybe that's more wrong information,' Andrew continued, and then remembered that his body had just been found.

'It might be someone else's,' wondered Clare aloud.

'No, no, it's definitely my father,' said Marjorie. 'I've read all the paperwork from the Swiss authorities.'

Marjorie explained that she'd found the two letters among her mother's papers after she'd died in 1974.

'And all these years you never said anything to us,' said Clare in amazement. 'Why not? I mean the whole thing's so extraordinary!' The letters had been a big surprise, but now she was beginning to find the whole mystery very interesting. And her opinion of her grandfather was quickly changing.

'There didn't seem any point – you never knew him and Grandma Agatha had always painted such a wonderful picture of her beloved Edward to you both – and to me too.'

'And do you know why he went to Zermatt?' asked Andrew.

'No, I only know what the letters say. But I can imagine that whatever the reason, it would have been a terrible thing for my mother to live with.' Marjorie went on, 'We're talking about the 1920s remember. Men didn't walk out on marriages like they do today. It would have been a scandal then. I should imagine she was almost happy when he was killed – at least she had a respectable reason for being alone with a child.'

Clare and Andrew listened as Marjorie talked about her feelings towards her mother. She'd found her death difficult to deal with – they'd had a very close relationship, probably because she was an only child, brought up without a father. She'd shown the letters to her husband, Thomas, and they'd decided it was better to keep the information to themselves. Of course they'd discussed all the possibilities of why Edward had gone – like a business scandal that had forced him to leave, or maybe he and Agatha were no longer able to live together for some reason.

'My mother was a demanding person, as you know. She

had incredibly high expectations. Maybe he felt he couldn't come up to her standards. I don't know,' said Marjorie rather sadly.

'Or maybe he had another woman,' said Clare. 'But why Zermatt?'

'Well, it was his favourite place I believe. They spent their honeymoon there and we went as a family in . . . let me see . . . 1922 or '23 – the summer before he died, so it must have been '23.'

'That's right,' said Andrew. 'I remember you telling us that ages ago. And when we were kids you told us about riding through the streets in a smart carriage pulled by white horses.'

'With red feathers on their heads,' added Clare. 'Yes, I remember that too. So Mum you *do* have some memories of that time, then.'

'Some unclear bits maybe. But to be honest I don't know if what I remember was real or maybe it's just what my mother told me and I've taken it as my own memory. You know how it is, it's all very confused,' said Marjorie, waving her hand as though it was not important. 'Anyway I've always believed he chose Zermatt because he liked it there and of course he loved the mountains – climbing.'

'I wonder if I'll find out any more when I go out there,' said Clare.

'I doubt it,' said her mother. 'It was all so long ago.' Then she looked at her daughter closely and added, 'And don't you go asking lots of questions, Clare. I know you – you never could stand a mystery. Always wanted to know why. Just let it rest, please.'

None of them slept particularly well that night. In three

separate bedrooms, three brains were thinking about the mystery of Edward Crowe.

The following morning, having booked her flight to Geneva for Tuesday, Clare drove back down to London, leaving Andrew to make arrangements with the local cemetery for a new addition to the family grave.

Chapter 6   *Arriving in Zermatt*

Clare's plane turned steeply as it started its approach to Geneva airport. She could see the tops of the mountains still covered in snow and wondered if she might have time to do a bit of skiing in Zermatt. Then she immediately felt guilty – this wasn't a holiday!

But she had to admit that she was quite excited about the developing family mystery. It was becoming even more interesting than simply having a grandfather who had fallen to his death on a mountain. There was now most definitely a skeleton in the family cupboard, a skeleton she knew she would not be able to ignore – unlike her mother.

She caught the train at Geneva Airport and sat back to enjoy the four-hour journey. As the train travelled round the Lake of Geneva the spring sunshine danced on the water, and in the lakeside gardens white flowers on the trees made Clare realise how far south she'd travelled since the weekend. Here spring was well advanced and the sun had real warmth.

The train slowly left the lake behind and turned towards the mountains. The scenery was in many ways very familiar to her – it was not that different from the Lake District, except everything was bigger. She could understand why her grandfather had liked it here. At Visp, Clare changed trains and began the long climb up the valley to Zermatt. She remembered this part from when she'd been before, even though it was over twenty years ago. It was a beautiful journey with the railway line keeping to the side of the mountain. Then, as it went round a corner, she saw the Matterhorn. The setting sun had bathed the whole thing in a pinky-orange light. It stood there in the distance all on its own, bright, almost as if it was on fire. Clare found herself thinking that if you had to die in a climbing accident, there could be many worse places to lie for seventy-four years.

She walked out of the station and was delighted to see that the smart carriages pulled by horses were still operating. There were two of them, obviously belonging to expensive hotels. She decided she would stay in one of them, if there was room. She wanted to ride in one of the carriages, just like her mother had. The Tourist Office told her there was a room at the Grand Hotel Zermatterhof. It was horribly expensive, but why not? She earned enough money. Why not spend some while she could.

The uniformed driver helped her into the closed carriage, and put her luggage in beside her. She was then taken up the main, car-free street of the town the whole magnificent distance of 300 metres to the front door of the hotel! As she walked in, her first thought was she hadn't brought enough smart clothes with her.

She registered at reception and was taken up to her room which had a south-facing balcony. There was just enough light and warmth left for her to sit on the balcony with a gin and tonic from the mini-bar and let her eyes take it all in. 'How lovely to be here,' she thought, 'even if it is for a rather strange reason. Business starts tomorrow. This evening is for me. Bath, dinner, and then bed with a book. Perfect!'

She went downstairs for dinner at eight o'clock. The head waiter took her from the door of the magnificent dining room to a table in the corner near a window. She sat there and looked around her. In the course of her work, and as a single woman, she had eaten in many hotels and restaurants on her own and she was very aware of where waiters seated her. She hated having a table in the middle of a room when she had her back to half the room. And she also hated being hidden away somewhere in some dark corner as if there was embarrassment in being a lone diner. But her table here was just right. This hotel knew its business.

After a huge dinner, she felt in need of a walk. Also she wasn't ready to go to bed yet – she wanted to explore Zermatt a little – get a feel for the place. There were lots of people walking up and down the main street, mainly looking in the shop windows. She joined in the general movement. In one office window she saw detailed maps of the three main skiing areas which showed that some of the higher ski runs were still open, particularly the ones in the Matterhorn area. She also identified several places where she could hire skis. Good, everything was working out well.

Having found the police station where she'd have to go tomorrow to start all the official business, she turned off the main street into the old part of the town. She remembered from her previous visit how interested she'd been by the store houses down here. And there they were, still. Wonderful old wooden buildings standing on what looked like tall stone mushrooms. They were built like this to keep the rats out of the food, she'd been told. She felt that this part of the town would have looked more or less the same in her grandfather's time – he might even have stayed down here. She could be walking in his footsteps. 'What was he like?' she wondered. 'Would I have enjoyed his company?' She certainly liked his choice of Zermatt.

There was a small bar almost hidden behind an old wooden house. She pushed open the heavy door and was met by a wall of heat and loud voices. She sat at the bar and started reading something she'd picked up in the Tourist Office. But the voices disturbed her. Most of them were German-speaking but from one table in the corner, English came across loud and clear.

'I wonder what condition he was in?'

'Frozen solid, I should think.'

'Doubt it. It's been quite warm these last two weeks. I should think he'd begun to melt.'

'Oh, Harry. What a disgusting thought!'

'Apparently his family are going to take him back to England.'

Clare realised with a shock that they were talking about her grandfather. Well, well . . . so his reappearance seemed to be common knowledge.

Chapter 7 *The first steps*

At breakfast the following morning Clare realised that she didn't like other people talking about her grandfather. It was a family matter and nobody else's business. She was also worried that if it was such common knowledge, then sooner or later some newspaper or magazine was going to start looking for a story. And Clare didn't like the idea of someone else using her story.

Clare walked into the police station and introduced herself. 'Good morning. My name is Clare Newton. I've come about my grandfather, Edward Crowe.'

'Good morning, Ms Newton. We were expecting you. Would you like to come this way, please?' The young receptionist, who spoke excellent English, led Clare into a modern office and introduced her to Herr Ziegler, who spoke less excellent English, but it was still better than her German.

Herr Ziegler explained that the body had been recovered yesterday and had been taken away for a post mortem examination. She looked at him in surprise.

'Is that normal – to do a post mortem when someone died so long ago?'

'Oh yes, quite normal. We must follow the rules,' said Herr Ziegler. 'We must confirm that this is indeed your grandfather, Edward Crowe.' He went on to say that if everything was in order, the paperwork could be completed quite quickly and that arrangements could be made for Clare and her grandfather to return to England, probably in about seven or eight days' time. In the meanwhile, Clare could 'take advantage of your little stay in Zermatt and enjoy the wonderful scenery'.

'And you must visit our Alpine Museum,' Herr Ziegler continued. 'There is much interesting information about climbing. Many photographs of old climbers who were killed on the mountains – maybe one of your grandfather?'

Clare thanked him, and decided that the Alpine Museum sounded as good a place as any to start getting a bit of background, and a bit of a feel for the time period when Edward Crowe lived in Zermatt.

The museum was very interesting. She read all about the first successful climb of the Matterhorn by an Englishman in 1865. She examined photos of enthusiastic looking young men from place like Britain, Italy and even the USA, who had died while climbing. Some of the photos had obviously been taken back in their own countries; others had been taken in Zermatt with the men dressed in their climbing clothes ready for action. She looked closely at them and wondered how anyone had managed to climb in clothes that were more suitable for a Sunday afternoon in the garden. Grandfather Edward was not there, however.

There *was* a photo of another Englishman, Gordon Younger, who had been killed in the same year, 1924, but no Edward Crowe. What a pity. She would have liked to see him hanging on the wall with all the other men whose lives had been shortened so suddenly.

On one wall of the museum there was another collection of photographs, this time of the local guides who'd taken these early foreign climbers up their mountains. Some of them had also died young, but others had faces that looked incredibly old, dark-skinned and lined, showing the outdoor lives they'd led. One guide with the most wonderful moustache was apparently still alive. There was a brief notice under his photo that said he'd started guiding in 1922 at the age of eighteen and had been up the Matterhorn for the last time in 1990.

'Good God,' thought Clare. 'He must be tough. He'd have been eighty-six when he went up then. That's incredible!'

Then she realised that he'd have been a guide during her grandfather's time. Maybe, even, had known Edward Crowe. She wrote down his name – Ulrich Grunwalder. She would like to talk to him, if he was still able to communicate.

Chapter 8   *Ulrich Grunwalder*

Back at the Zermatterhof there was a message from Kevin for her at reception. Call him back a.s.a.p. He always put 'as soon as possible' on his messages – just to make things sound urgent, and it annoyed her. She decided she wouldn't call him back as soon as possible – she'd go and have lunch instead. She found a café down by the river with tables outside. She sat in the sun and had lovely potato *rösti* with two fried eggs on top.

Later that afternoon, after more messages from Kevin had arrived, she rang him back.

'Hi, babe! What news?' Kevin said cheerfully.

'Do you mind, Kevin!' replied Clare angrily. 'Don't call me "babe". I'm old enough to be your mother.'

'You said it babe . . . sorry . . . I mean Clare.'

'You sound cheerful. What's happened? Have we been bought by some amazingly wonderful person who will allow us to write about real issues, or are you just pleased to talk to me?'

'Very funny,' answered Kevin. 'I just wanted to know how things were going. First of all, what about your interview with Cherry Gaskell?'

'No problem. Fixed for ten days' time. She was quite pleased to have more time, I think,' said Clare.

'And how's your grandpa? Any news there?'

'Like what?' replied Clare a little too quickly.

'I dunno – like maybe his death wasn't an accident, that maybe he was pushed.'

'You'd like that, wouldn't you? Look, I've told you, this is a private story – not for the newspaper.' But Clare knew that it was a good story and that somebody would publish it – even if it wasn't the *Daily News*.

'We've printed a little bit in today's paper – just giving the facts you know . . .'

'Kevin, you bastard!' said Clare.

'Come on, Clare. How long have you been in the business? You can't honestly think I'd miss the chance of a good story. Look, if you do it, you can write it in the way you want – I promise. Surely that must be better than some stranger writing it – you know how reporters get things wrong.' Kevin laughed.

And Clare knew he was right, but she didn't tell him.

*   *   *

That afternoon Clare made some enquiries about Ulrich Grunwalder and discovered he was still alive, in good health and still to be seen wandering around the old part of Zermatt most afternoons. She also learnt that he could speak some English – probably as a result of taking English people climbing, she thought. So she decided that she too would wander around Zermatt that afternoon, in the hope of seeing him. There couldn't be many ninety-four-year-olds still out and about, so surely she would be able to identify him. If not, she could always try arranging an appointment through more normal channels – like the Tourist Office.

She spent a very pleasant hour exploring all the small streets between the river and the new part of town. The planning authorities, or whoever, had really done a good job in preserving the character of the old town. There were even some houses with the traditional animal quarters attached. She looked in one and saw some goats, and in another some sheep. They all seemed a bit restless.

'They can smell the spring,' said a voice behind her.

She turned round and there was Ulrich Grunwalder. At least she presumed it was him. He was a small man, very bent, with a face like leather and a huge, thick moustache – and incredibly old-looking.

'Oh,' said Clare in surprise, then recovered. 'Yes, they do seem to want to be in the fresh air, don't they?'

By the time she'd finished her sentence, Herr Grunwalder had started to move away. She followed him.

'Herr Grunwalder?' she said, and he turned round. 'Herr Grunwalder. May I talk to you for a moment?' asked Clare.

'Of course,' he replied. 'We will sit over there,' and he pointed to a wooden seat on the corner.

'You speak very good English,' said Clare trying to speak clearly without shouting.

'Yes. I learnt it from English people. When I was a guide, you know.' His voice trembled a bit, and he spoke quietly so Clare had to lean forward to hear what he was saying.

'I saw your photograph in the museum and I wanted to meet you to ask you about your life,' said Clare.

'Why do you want to know about me?' asked the old man looking at her with his still, grey eyes.

'I'm a writer,' said Clare. Something stopped her from saying she was a journalist. She felt that Herr Grunwalder, for some reason, might not like journalists. 'And I'm here to study mountaineering in the early part of this century, particularly from the point of view of the young Englishmen who came out here to climb.' Well at least that part was true, she thought.

'Ah yes, the English – so many of them.' Ulrich Grunwalder turned away from her and looked into the distance towards the Matterhorn. 'They were the first, you know. They were very keen to climb our famous mountain. Then all the others followed – the Americans, the Germans. It was an exciting time to be young.'

The old man sat perfectly still, his hands resting on his walking stick in front of him, his thoughts re-living his memories. Clare felt very comfortable with his silence. She too could imagine how exciting it must have been for a young Zermatter to meet all those people from foreign lands – places that people from a small mountain village might never even have heard of. She could also imagine that these people from the outside world must have disturbed the traditional way of life and brought changes that were not welcomed by everyone.

'Do you know anything about this Englishman's body they've just recovered?' asked Clare, breaking the silence.

Herr Grunwalder answered her slowly, 'I've heard something about it.'

'His name was Edward Crowe. He died in 1924 on that mountain,' said Clare pointing to the Matterhorn. 'Did you know him?'

'No . . . there were so many.' He then raised himself to his feet with the help of his stick and walked away.

Chapter 9   *Ulrich's early life*

Zermatt, August 1923.

19-year-old Ulrich lay down to rest. It was a hot day and he'd been working all morning in the family fields high above the village. The sheep and cows were spread over a wide area, enjoying their freedom. Ulrich had spent the morning carrying huge bundles of dry grass on his back uphill to the summer hut. There his mother and sister were busy making the cheese that would last the family throughout the winter.

The sun was strong and he was tired. He raised his head slightly and looked over towards the Matterhorn. His friend, Otto, was up there, guiding two American climbers. Ulrich went into the hut and got the binoculars. He thought that Otto might possibly have reached the 'shoulder' by now – one of the most difficult places to climb on the whole mountain. He thought he could see three little dots – yes, they were definitely moving.

Ulrich's heart was racing as he watched their slow progress. He wished he was up there with them. It was a perfect day for climbing. He himself had been a guide for a year now and had climbed to the top five times. He knew that however many times he was going to climb the Matterhorn in the future he would never tire of it. It was different from all the other mountains around; not just because it was so high but because it was the most magnificent and mysterious. His ancestors had believed that the mountain was sacred, that the gods lived there and so it was an unvisited place. Since it had been first climbed in 1865, many people had lost their lives on it, including his father four years ago.

Ulrich had started climbing with his father – the most respected guide of his generation in Zermatt. It was quite normal for fathers and sons to work together, and Grunwalder Senior was pleased that his son would soon be old enough to join him, guiding the wealthy foreigners up the high mountains. This dream had been cut short when Grunwalder Senior had died helping a not very experienced Englishman come down the 'shoulder' of the Matterhorn. The whole village had come together for the funeral of his father. He was buried, with all the other local guides who had met a similar end, in a special corner of the cemetery near the church. His father's death had not changed Ulrich's mind – he too wanted to be the most respected guide of his generation. He also knew that as the only male in the family it was his duty to provide for his mother and his sister, Marianne, until she got married, so he needed as much work as possible.

'Uli . . . Essen!' Marianne had crept up beside him with a plate of bread and cheese.

He jumped, and took the plate from his sister. Ulrich, Marianne and their mother sat together on the grass eating their lunch. Twenty-three-year-old Marianne suddenly announced that she was going back down to the village later that afternoon. Her cousin, who managed one of the hotels, wanted her to look after the little daughter of one of the guest families for a few days. Ulrich looked in surprise at his sister. It was unusual for Marianne to leave the hillside hut in the summer, unless she really had to. She was the one person in the family who particularly loved their summer life away from the village. Every year she used to cry when they brought the animals down from the uplands at the end of the summer. She saw it as the end of her own freedom; she would be stuck in the house in the village for the long months of the dark, cold winter.

'Why are you looking at me like that?' asked Marianne.

'You've surprised me,' said Ulrich. 'Did you know she was going, Mama?'

His mother nodded.

'Well, this little girl must be very special, or Cousin Hermann must be very persuasive, or something,' said Ulrich, noticing that his sister was now embarrassed.

'Don't be silly,' replied Marianne. 'You know we can get good tips from the foreign guests. I can't turn down the chance to earn some money. All the visitors will be gone in a couple of months and that'll be that – until next year.'

'I'm probably going to be working next week – there's an Englishman who wants to do some climbing on the Gornergrat so we'll get some money from that.' Ulrich felt the responsibility for providing money for the family was his. 'You don't need to do this for Cousin Hermann if you don't want to,' he added. 'I know how much you hate going down to the village in the summer.'

'Thank you, Uli, but I've said I'll do it, and I will.'

'Well, if you're both going to be away, I shall have a bit of peace up here for a few days,' said their mother.

'I'll walk back with you,' said Ulrich to his sister. 'I want to make sure that Englishman is really serious about climbing next week. And if he is, I don't want him to employ any other guide. Is that all right with you, Mama? I'll be back tomorrow morning.'

'Of course. And take as much hay down as possible, both of you,' replied his mother.

Later that afternoon, Ulrich and Marianne tied large bundles of hay together and lifted them onto their backs. They set off down towards Zermatt. An hour and a half later they entered the village, left the hay under their house and walked to their cousin's hotel, the Monte Rosa. Ulrich knew that he would be able to find his English mountaineer there; the Hotel Monte Rosa was the meeting place for the English gentlemen climbers, and was the place where the local guides were hired and many climbs were planned.

Cousin Hermann greeted them. Ulrich and Marianne both walked over to the English family sitting in the lounge – Mr and Mrs Crowe and their little daughter, Marjorie. It was only then that they realised they were both going to be employed by the same person.

Chapter 10 *Edward Crowe*

Zermatt, August 1923.

Edward Crowe introduced Ulrich to his wife, Agatha, and to his daughter. To Ulrich's surprise, Marianne seemed to know them already. 'Now Marjorie,' said Mrs Crowe to her small daughter, 'here's Marianne again. You remember her, don't you? She's going to be with us for a few days so your father can go climbing and I can do some painting.'

Marjorie smiled at Marianne and took her hand. Marianne then amazed Ulrich once more by saying a few words to the little girl in English. He made some comment, in his own language, to his sister about her ability to speak this foreign language, and she told him she had started learning it from a book last winter.

Edward Crowe was looking first at Ulrich and then at Marianne.

'This is my sister,' said Ulrich, realising that Mr Crowe hadn't quite made the connection.

'Well, well, what a coincidence.' He laughed. 'Isn't that odd, my dear?' said Edward to his wife.

'Not really,' she replied. 'Zermatt is a very small world. Anyway, Edward, we are going to leave you now to discuss your business with Herr Grunwalder. Come along Marjorie. Marianne is going to give you your tea and put you to bed.'

She shook hands with Ulrich, turned and walked across

the lounge with Marianne and Marjorie following. Both men watched the group disappear into the lift.

'I didn't know you had met my sister before,' said Ulrich to Edward Crowe.

'Yes, indeed. My wife and I met her three years ago when we came here to the Hotel Monte Rosa on our honeymoon. And of course we met again when we arrived this summer. Marjorie likes her very much. But enough of that, let's talk about our climb next week.'

Ulrich and his English mountaineer discussed the route for their climb up the Gornergrat. Ulrich was pleased that Mr Crowe had had quite a lot of climbing experience. The Gornergrat was not such a high mountain but they would be climbing on a glacier and this needed great care. It was agreed that Ulrich would come to the Monte Rosa on Tuesday evening to confirm that the climb was going ahead the following day. They would start very early on the Wednesday morning and be away for two days. Edward offered the standard fee for Ulrich's services which he was happy to accept, knowing that there would also be a tip at the end if the expedition was successful. They shook hands on the deal and parted.

Ulrich went to find his cousin Hermann and have a beer with him in the bar used by the locals. He was curious to find out about the Crowe family and how well Marianne knew them, but decided not to bother asking any questions when the two of them were joined by some of the other local men.

'So, you're going to be working for Mr Crowe next week then,' said one of the older men, Gottfried.

'That's right. Up the Gornergrat,' replied Ulrich, smiling

to himself at how quickly news travelled.

'Good climber. Very determined.'

'How do you know?' asked Ulrich.

'Climbed with him when he was here before,' said Gottfried, putting tobacco in his pipe.

'Why didn't he employ you again then, instead of using me?' Ulrich knew that satisfied customers were very faithful to their guides, so he was curious at this switch by Edward Crowe.

'Had a bit of a disagreement. We were on the Matterhorn, he wanted to carry on climbing, I said no, the weather was changing. I won, he didn't like it.' Gottfried added more tobacco to his pipe, and lit it. 'Good luck,' he added.

Some of the other guides were listening to this exchange and nodding – maybe they'd heard Gottfried's story before or maybe they were remembering similar experiences they'd had with clients who thought that because they were paying, they had the final word. Ulrich knew from his father that this was dangerous ground.

He also knew that there were ways of getting the message across to clients without being rude to them. And Gottfried, despite his climbing ability, said exactly what he thought, and didn't care how it sounded. Still, he'd have to be careful next week.

Nothing more was said about Edward Crowe. Ulrich stayed a little longer, mainly listening to the stories of the older guides and adding any useful bits of information to his store of knowledge.

In the days that followed, Ulrich and his mother worked in the fields. He made several more trips down to the village with hay for the animals in winter. On one occasion he saw Marianne walking down the main street with little Marjorie and Edward Crowe. All three of them were laughing about something together. Ulrich didn't disturb them.

The following Wednesday, in the early morning when most of the village was still asleep, he walked over to the Hotel Monte Rosa. There he found Edward Crowe ready and waiting. They set off as the sky was beginning to lighten. It was two months after the longest day, and the dawn was noticeably later now. Another reminder that autumn was approaching. They walked together in silence for a while.

The further they went on, however, the more relaxed Mr Crowe seemed to get. Whenever they stopped for a rest or to admire the view, Ulrich was asked questions about the area – the names of the different mountains, birds, plants – and about his life in Zermatt. Ulrich, not normally a talkative man, was affected by the obvious enthusiasm of Edward Crowe. That evening, in a mountain hut built for climbers, Ulrich listened to Edward Crowe talking about the area of England where he came from. To him, the Lake District sounded a familiar sort of place and again he realised how much Edward Crowe loved mountains and climbing. And he understood this feeling because he felt it too.

The following day, after another early start, they successfully climbed to the top of the Gornergrat and were even able to continue to the next mountain, Hohtalli. It had been Mr Crowe's suggestion that they should go on and Ulrich was happy to agree. The weather was fine and in Ulrich's judgement there was enough time to complete the climb and get back down to Zermatt before dark. He recognised the determination in Mr Crowe that Gottfried had mentioned, but felt it was acceptable on this occasion.

His judgement was right. The expedition was completed successfully. Both days had provided excellent climbing and Ulrich delivered a very satisfied customer back to the Monte Rosa that evening. Marianne was walking across the hall as they entered the hotel. Ulrich thought how attractive she looked as she smiled a welcome to them both. The two men went into the bar, Ulrich received his agreed fee and, as he had hoped, a considerable tip.

'Thank you, Ulrich, for your work. We made a good team, I believe,' said Mr Crowe, shaking Ulrich firmly by the hand. 'Next year I intend to come back for the summer and I would like to climb the Matterhorn. I want you to be my guide. Would you be agreeable to this?'

'Of course. I will be happy to climb with you again,' replied Ulrich. 'You are leaving Zermatt now?'

'At the end of the week. I must return to my work, and Mrs Crowe is missing her home. She and Marjorie may not come with me next year, we shall see.' Mr Crowe seemed to be thinking about another life in another world, but he wished Ulrich a good winter and said goodbye.

Life returned to normal for Ulrich and Marianne after the Crowes had left for England. At the end of the summer they brought the animals down from the upland fields to their winter quarters in the village. And, as usual, Marianne cried.

All the animals belonging to the village were being brought down during that week, so Zermatt became used to seeing well fed, healthy looking cows – some of them decorated with wild flowers and bells – coming down the main street.

But Ulrich was worried about his sister, and he noticed his mother looking at her rather sharply on one or two occasions. She had seemed unusually quiet over the last few weeks. When he mentioned something about it to his mother, she had said, 'It's time she got married. She's twenty-three. She needs her own family to look after. We must try to arrange a suitable husband for her this winter, Uli. Your father would have done it by now.'

So, one morning in November when he was at home with Marianne, he asked her if she wanted to get married, and if she had any feelings for any of the young unmarried men in the village. Marianne turned to him, her face pale and said in a quiet voice, 'No, I have no feelings for any of the Zermatt men. Only for the Englishman, Mr Crowe.' And immediately burst into tears.

Chapter 11 *Andrew calls*

Clare suspected that the name Edward Crowe meant something to Ulrich Grunwalder, despite what he'd said. She watched him disappear into one of the old houses, and knew she had to find out more about this old man.

She tried at her hotel reception on her return.

'I've just met Ulrich Grunwalder. What a wonderful old man he is,' said Clare.

'Yes. He's amazing, isn't he?' answered the receptionist. 'Zermatters are very proud of him – he was the best mountain guide for about forty years. All the mountaineers who came here to climb the Matterhorn used to ask for him.'

'Does he belong to one of the old Zermatt families?'

'Oh yes. The Grunwalders have been in this valley for centuries,' the receptionist continued. 'If you look in the cemetery you'll find lots of them buried there. And of course, they are still here. He's got two sons and lots of grandchildren around him. The family owns quite a lot of the property in Zermatt.'

'You know why I'm here, I'm sure,' said Clare, knowing that village talk travels fast. 'It's my grandfather who has come out of the glacier.'

'Yes, I heard about it. Well, to be honest, everyone's talking about it,' the receptionist replied.

'Do you think Herr Grunwalder might have known my

grandfather? After all, there can't have been many English climbers around at that time,' asked Clare innocently. 'It's possible, I suppose, that he might even have been his guide.'

'Possibly. You'd have to ask him, or maybe they'd be able to help at the Alpine Museum. I know they've got records of a lot of the climbs. Yes, why don't you ask there? But you must excuse me.' The receptionist smiled and moved away to deal with another guest.

Clare went up to her room to have a bath and change for dinner. She had a feeling that as soon as she got into the bath the telephone would ring, and it would be Kevin demanding to know what was happening. So she rang down to reception and asked them not to put anyone through for half an hour. She wanted a relaxing bath and a read of the book she'd just bought about Zermatt at the beginning of the century.

Thirty minutes later, and a quick look at her alarm clock told her that it was precisely that, the phone rang. But it wasn't Kevin, it was her brother Andrew.

'How's it going?' Andrew's voice sounded very distant, which Clare thought must be the line.

'OK, Andrew. The police here seem to have got everything organised. They're doing a post mortem at the moment and . . .'

'So grandfather's out of the ice, then?' said Andrew.

'Yeah . . . yesterday, or the day before, I don't know exactly. Anyway, all the paperwork and so on should be done in a few days. And then we'll come home. How's Mum?'

'Seems fine. I haven't seen her but she sounds OK on the

phone. Talking about everything else except her father, of course,' said Andrew. 'By the way, Clare, there was a short piece in your paper about Edward Crowe's reappearance and his granddaughter who just happens to work for the same paper.'

Andrew's voice sounded very cold, and Clare felt bad.

'That was Kevin. He did it without my knowledge,' said Clare, truthfully. 'Honestly, Andrew, I told him it was a private family matter and to keep his hands off it. But he doesn't care. To him, if it sells newspapers, that's fine – just print it and move on to the next story. You know what he's like.'

'Yeah. But what are *you* like, Clare?' Andrew asked quickly.

'Oh Andrew, don't ask,' said Clare sadly. 'I'm in an impossible situation.' She explained about their grandfather's reappearance being common knowledge and how the story was certain to be picked up by journalists anyway, and how she felt that in the end it might be better, and more accurate, if she did agree to write it.

'Mm,' said Andrew doubtfully. 'Well just remember it's not only your story, it's mine and Mum's too. So make sure Kevin doesn't change it.'

Clare told him not to worry.

'Have you heard anything about how he died yet?' Andrew asked.

'Not yet,' she replied, 'but I think I will.' And Clare went on to tell him about her meeting with Ulrich Grunwalder.

'Interesting,' said Andrew. Clare could hear someone shouting Andrew's name in the background – Jan, she supposed. 'Anyway, Clare, keep in touch and more importantly keep Kevin under control.'

'I will,' replied Clare. 'Love to Jan and the kids.'

As soon as she put the phone down, it rang again. This time it was Kevin, but she couldn't face talking to him, so she told him that there was nothing to report. She didn't want to tell him that she would write her grandfather's story for the paper – she didn't want to give him the pleasure of knowing that he'd won – again.

She took her Zermatt book down to dinner. The more she read, the more interested she became in the place and why her grandfather had come here. She was excited at the thought of discovering who her grandfather really was and what made him behave as he did. She realised it had become important to find out everything, not just for the story but for herself.

Meanwhile, Ulrich Grunwalder was sitting at home remembering very clearly the times when Edward Crowe came to Zermatt, and wishing he could forget.

Chapter 12 *Past and present*

The next morning, Clare decided to go back to the Alpine Museum to see if they had any records of her grandfather's climb up the Matterhorn.

In her best German, she tried to explain to the woman selling tickets what she wanted, but obviously her best German was not good enough as the woman just kept shaking her head.

'Can I help you?' said a voice in English. A man appeared at her elbow.

'Well, I was trying to find out from this lady whether the museum had any records, or climbing diaries, or anything of the early Matterhorn expeditions,' said Clare turning to this man gratefully. The man spoke quickly to the woman and then put his hand under Clare's elbow and led her towards an open door at the back of the small museum. He introduced himself as Roland Kronig, manager of the museum and said they did have some records, not complete by any means, and then asked when she was interested in.

'1924,' she said as Herr Kronig unlocked a cupboard on the far wall.

'1924 . . . 1924,' he echoed. 'Here's something dated 1924, July 1924, but not the Matterhorn. You did say the Matterhorn, didn't you?'

'Yes.' Clare was beginning to feel excited.

'I'm afraid there seems to be nothing for 1924 for the

Matterhorn. That's unusual, I must say. We do have something for most years. But of course, in those days there was no organisation that kept official records of climbers and their expeditions. Not like now.' Herr Kronig smiled at her. 'The ones that we have were given to us, or found in the Hotel Monte Rosa which, as I am sure you know, was where all the mountaineers met in the early days.'

Clare remembered the photo she'd seen on her first visit to the museum of the Englishman who'd died on the Matterhorn in 1924. What was his name . . . George . . . Gordon . . . ?

'There's a photo in one of the rooms of an Englishman who died on the Matterhorn in 1924. What was his name?' asked Clare.

'I'm not sure – there were so many who came to climb. Perhaps you would like to show me?'

Clare led the way to the room and pointed to the photograph of Gordon Younger.

'Ah yes, Gordon Younger,' said Herr Kronig. 'A bit of a mystery there. We don't know very much about him. All we know is that he was climbing with another man and they both died. But only one body was recovered. The name of the other man was never known.'

'And would they have been climbing with a local guide, do you think?' asked Clare.

'Almost certainly. But in this case, history does not tell us who it was,' replied Herr Kronig.

'Isn't that a bit strange?' said Clare with surprise. 'Surely someone in such a small community would have known even if there was no official record?'

'I'm sure they did at the time. But for some reason the name seems to have been forgotten over the years.' Herr Kronig stood there politely waiting to see if he could help this foreign visitor any more. Clare thanked him and turned to leave.

'Madame,' said Herr Kronig. 'If you want to find out more about the Matterhorn in the 1920s, the only thing I can suggest is that you talk to Ulrich Grunwalder. He was around at that time.'

She left the Museum disappointed, but with the definite feeling that Ulrich Grunwalder was the person she needed to speak to. She felt that with time and a bit of patient questioning from her, he would be able to remember something about the accident in 1924.

But the sun was shining and Clare felt like doing something active. She'd had enough for the moment of living in the past. What she really wanted was some skiing if she could get herself organised. She walked into the ski school office and within ten minutes had arranged a private class for the whole afternoon. One of the ski teachers would meet her at the ski lift station at the end of the village at midday. The ski hire shop next door rented her some skis and boots and she carried them back to the hotel. There she changed into some more or less suitable clothes and took the hotel's electric taxi down to the lift station. She was a bit early and had time to look around, and get nervous. She hadn't skied for about ten years, though she'd been quite good then. Everyone said it was like riding a bike – you didn't forget how to do it. She stood there looking up at the mountains, trying to remember what to do.

'Madame Newton?'

'Yes,' she said. And there was her ski teacher, looking exactly like all the other ski teachers she remembered – sun-tanned, handsome and totally self-confident.

Half an hour later all thoughts of Ulrich Grunwalder and Edward Crowe had disappeared as she skied behind Bruno and concentrated on staying on her feet.

'Upper body still, make your legs do the work, Madame,' shouted Bruno over his shoulder.

'Clare,' she said. 'Call me Clare, please.'

'Clare. OK. Lean forward a bit more, Clare. That's it. Good. You are remembering now, eh?'

'Yeah, I am . . . slowly. It's great. I'd forgotten what an amazing buzz skiing gives you.'

They skied down some different runs with Bruno being wonderfully encouraging, and she really did begin to feel confident on the skis. Going up in the lifts, Clare and Bruno chatted – just the usual 'where are you from, what do you do' sort of chat, but it was pleasantly relaxing. In the middle of the afternoon, they stopped at an old farmhouse for coffee and apple cake. There were lots of other skiers doing the same. Clare felt as if she belonged – something about being part of a group, all with a shared interest, she supposed. It was a feeling she'd not had for a long time.

Bruno said hello to a few people, and went over to talk to one of the waiters. Clare took the opportunity to study him a bit. Up until now, she'd just been skiing behind a man in a red ski suit, so it was interesting to see that he was quite tall, with curly brown hair and eyes to match. From the colour of his face he looked as if he'd spent his whole life in the open air. She guessed he was about forty.

'Are you in Zermatt for long, Clare?' asked Bruno, after he'd been sitting with her a few minutes.

'No, only a few days probably. Just a short break to get away from everything at home,' replied Clare. She didn't feel like explaining the real reason. People looked at her differently when they knew. 'But I'd like to do some more skiing. Would you be able to do anything tomorrow?'

'I think so. But you'll have to book it through the Ski School office. I can't arrange anything with you directly,' said Bruno, putting on his gloves and standing up. 'Come on. Let's do a bit more now.'

'Great,' replied Clare.

After another hour, Clare said, 'Time to stop, I think.'

Bruno agreed. 'You should have a sauna tonight. It'll help your body relax. Not so stiff tomorrow, you know.'

Clare didn't care how stiff she was going to be tomorrow. She felt better than she had done for months – full of fresh air, physically tired but in her mind – alive. Happy! Yes, that was how she felt – happy!

At the bottom of the lift where she'd met Bruno a few hours earlier, they shook hands.

'See you tomorrow, I hope,' said Clare.

'Yes, I hope so. But would you like to meet for a drink later? After dinner?' Bruno was looking at her directly and smiling confidently.

'That'd be nice,' she replied immediately. 'Where?'

'There's a bar in the Hotel Monte Rosa, just opposite your hotel. We could meet there at, say, half past nine?'

'OK, see you later then.' Clare walked off towards the hotel taxi with a huge grin on her face.

Chapter 13 *A night out*

'Do you do this often?' asked Clare in the Monte Rosa bar later that evening.

'What, drink in this bar?' replied Bruno.

'No, invite your clients for a drink after the first lesson? Is it part of the service?'

'Sometimes I do, but not often, no. It depends. I just thought it'd be a nice way to spend an evening. Seemed like a normal thing to do, really. No?'

'Yes, perfectly normal,' replied Clare quickly. 'And much more interesting for me than staying in my hotel all evening.'

'Well, that's fine then.' Bruno laughed. And she began to relax.

In the course of the next couple of hours, and a bottle of wine, they discovered that they had a fair amount in common. They were both divorced (but he had kids), neither of them was looking for another serious commitment – or so they said, and for different reasons they both felt dissatisfied with their lives.

'I look at my father,' said Bruno, 'and I think, my life is the same as his. He was a ski teacher and so am I, and a mountain guide in the summer and so am I. OK, I've travelled a lot more than he has, but it depresses me to think that I haven't made more of my life. I look at him and see myself in thirty years' time.'

'Most people from the outside world would think you had a perfect lifestyle,' said Clare.

'Yeah, but they only see it for short amounts of time. Oh, I don't know. I like what I do, but is this all there is to life?' Bruno looked at her over his glass and saw she was looking a bit sad. He poured some more wine into her glass and apologised. 'Sorry. You came here to get away from real life. I didn't mean to start talking about all that.'

'It's difficult not to – unless we talk about the weather, or skiing or the snow conditions or something like that,' replied Clare. 'Anyway, you're talking to someone of more or less the same age – remember? I understand exactly how you're feeling, so don't apologise. I've been asking myself "What next?" for a while – but *that* I don't want to talk about.'

'OK. Look, you wouldn't like a dance, would you? There's quite a good club near here. I feel like doing something my father wouldn't do,' laughed Bruno.

'I haven't been to a club for ages, but why not?' said Clare, brightening up.

One or two of the locals watched with interest as Bruno and Clare left the bar together. The nightclub was crowded and the dance floor even more so. She was surprised to see that most people were dancing together in couples, rather than disco dancing which was what she'd been expecting. But it was fun. She found herself thinking that dancing with a partner was quite sexy – hands and bodies touching in interesting ways.

'I'm enjoying this,' said Bruno, echoing her thoughts.

'Mmm,' said Clare into his chest, where her head just happened to be resting.

In between dances Clare entertained him with stories about her London life. She told him she worked for a newspaper but didn't go into much detail. But she did tell him about some of the people she'd interviewed and about some of the funny things that had happened in the course of her job. Bruno seemed to like her stories and they spent a lot of the evening laughing.

It was after two when they eventually left the club. It seemed natural for Bruno to put his arm round Clare as they strolled down the main street towards the Zermatterhof. They talked quietly all the way back. At the entrance to the hotel, they turned towards each other. Clare leaned forward and Bruno kissed her on both cheeks and then very lightly on the lips.

'Thanks for . . .' said Clare and Bruno at the same time.

'Thanks for a wonderful evening,' laughed Clare.

'No, thank *you*. I haven't enjoyed myself so much for ages,' replied Bruno. 'We're OK for tomorrow afternoon's skiing – you fixed it with the ski school, didn't you?'

'Yes – if I'm still standing after all this exercise,' said Clare.

'See you at the lift station at twelve then. Goodnight and thanks again.'

'You're more than welcome,' said Clare to herself as she walked upstairs to her bedroom.

Chapter 14   *Information*

On Friday morning Clare woke surprisingly early and with a huge appetite. She got out of bed immediately, and tested her body – a bit stiff in the top half of the legs but not bad really. And no headache from last night's drinking – good, must be the clean air. She helped herself to breakfast in the dining room and thought about last night. She'd had a good time but wondered if she'd made a fool of herself. A handsome ski teacher invites woman on her own for a drink – it was a bit of a cliché. Oh well, we'll see later on, she thought, after I've been to the police station.

Herr Ziegler received her in his office and said that the post mortem results had shown that the body was that of her grandfather, Edward Crowe.

'Would it be possible for me to see him?' asked Clare.

Herr Ziegler looked surprised. 'I do not think it is a very good idea, Madame. You know after seventy years under the ice it is not in good condition. He is very dried up, I'm sorry to say.'

'Yes, of course,' said Clare. 'I wasn't thinking.'

'We found a wallet in the pocket of his jacket.' Herr Ziegler opened a drawer in his desk and brought out a plastic envelope in which there was a dark-looking object. 'His name was on the inside of the wallet. And there was also a photograph.' He handed it to her and she gasped. It was a photograph of her mother, aged about three. She recognised it immediately because it was the same one that she had in her house in London.

'You know this person?' asked Herr Ziegler.

'Yes, it's my mother,' said Clare, a bit shakily. 'Can I keep these things?' she asked.

'Yes, we have finished with them now,' replied Herr Ziegler. 'But I must ask you to sign this paper to say that they have been given to you. Could you please write your name . . . just here.' Herr Ziegler pointed to a space on the paper and Clare signed.

'We have done everything we need, Madame Newton. We will arrange for your grandfather's body to be transported to Geneva airport with all the correct paperwork. Would it be all right for you to fly back to England on Monday or Tuesday?'

'Yes, that's fine. I'll go back to my hotel and make all the arrangements,' said Clare. 'By the way, I took up your suggestion of going to the Alpine Museum. It's a very interesting place – a bit sad in some ways, all those young lives lost.'

'Yes, but they died doing something that they loved, I believe.'

'True,' said Clare. 'Anyway, unfortunately I was not able to get any more information from the museum about how my grandfather died. There was no record of the climb there, nobody seems to know who he was climbing with or anything.'

'That is a pity. But I am surprised they did not know his climbing partner. I have heard that he was climbing with another Englishman who also died. His name was Gordon Young, I believe.'

'Gordon Younger, you mean?' asked Clare excitedly.

'Yes, yes, Gordon Younger. That is right. He . . .'

'Herr Ziegler,' Clare interrupted, 'how do you know that he was with Gordon Younger?'

'It is just something that everybody has always said. Mr Crowe and Mr Younger were together. They both died but Mr Younger's body was brought down. He is buried in the cemetery. But the rescue people couldn't reach your grandfather. This is the story that is believed in the village.'

'And do you know the name of the guide they were climbing with? Was it Ulrich Grunwalder?' asked Clare.

'That, I do not know,' said Herr Ziegler.

'Well, thank you for the information,' said Clare. She stood up to leave. 'I'll ring you later this morning about which flight I'll take next week. Goodbye, and thank you again.'

Clare left the police station feeling confused. The photograph of her mother which had lain in Edward Crowe's wallet for all those years made him more of a real person to her. He had so obviously cared about the little daughter he had left behind. How sad that he would never see her again. In her mind, Clare saw him as an adventurous, rather romantic man who was searching for something. But maybe she was wrong, maybe he was a selfish individual who had destroyed his family. She wanted answers to her questions; she wanted a more complete picture of her grandfather.

And now she had one answer – the name of his climbing companion. It was strange that no-one had been able to tell her this before. She'd certainly asked the right questions of the right people. It almost seemed as if some people didn't want her to know – but why? She couldn't see any reason for it being a secret – it all happened so long ago.

Back at the hotel, she confirmed her flight home for Monday and then made herself ring Kevin. She had to let him know she was going to write the story.

'Hi, babe,' said Kevin. 'I was just going to ring you. What news?'

'Kevin, do you call me "babe" to annoy me, because you certainly succeed?' asked Clare

'Oh, don't be so sensitive,' laughed Kevin. 'Look, I need something from you for tomorrow's paper, otherwise the story'll go cold.'

'OK, babe.' Clare replied sharply, but then realised that Kevin would probably like being called that – he'd think it made him young and sexy. Some hope! 'The story is that Grandfather is coming home on Monday on Swissair flight 354, landing Heathrow at three in the afternoon.'

'Right. We'll get a photographer there,' said Kevin. 'Anything else? I need something more personal, more special, more intimate – you're his granddaughter, you can give me a bit more.'

Clare told him about the photograph of her mother found on Edward's body and also that he'd been climbing with another Englishman who'd also died.

'Look, I think we should just run a short article tomorrow and save the full story for next Tuesday,' said Clare. 'I'll e-mail through something for tomorrow as soon as I put the phone down.'

'OK. I'll go with that. And next week's article will be full-page with lots of detail about the accident, how your mother feels etc. Have you talked to the family of the man he was climbing with? That might be another side to the story. And what about . . . ?' Clare interrupted him.

'Stop trying to teach me my job. I'll write the article the way I want. But you'll have it in time for the Tuesday paper, and it'll be good.'

'It'd better be,' replied Kevin. 'By the way, have you come across any other journalists out there?'

'No, why?' asked Clare.

'There was a short paragraph about your grandfather in today's *Morning Times*. Just reporting the facts.'

'They may not have anyone out here, they may just have picked it up from Reuters or one of the other news agencies,' said Clare.

'Mmm, possible,' agreed Kevin. 'But keep your eyes and ears open for anyone else asking questions. I want to be first on this story.'

'OK. Is that it for now?' asked Clare.

'Yep. Send that story through now, will you? And ring me again over the weekend at the office – I'm on duty this weekend,' said Kevin.

By the time Clare had e-mailed her article, she'd already decided her next line of approach on the Ulrich Grunwalder question. Bruno. He was a mountain guide, he must surely know Ulrich Grunwalder. Maybe she could get Bruno to fix a meeting with him, or maybe he himself would know something about her grandfather's accident. In any case, she was going to have to tell him why she was in Zermatt if she wanted his help. She hoped this wouldn't change what was promising to be an interesting friendship.

Chapter 15 *With Bruno's help*

'Clare! Just let the skis run across the ice! Don't fight it!'
called Bruno over his shoulder.

They were skiing in a different place from yesterday and
Clare was not enjoying it. It was quite a bit steeper and
there was too much ice. Every time Clare tried to ski over
it, she lost control. She felt like a beginner all over again.

She fell on one particularly large area of ice and found
herself sliding head first down the mountain. Both her skis
had come off.

'Swing your legs round,' shouted Bruno. 'Use your feet
to stop yourself.'

She managed to stop when it became less steep, but lay
there for a moment without moving. Looking up the
mountain, she saw Bruno skiing down and carrying her
skis.

'You OK?' he asked. 'That was quite a long fall.'

'Yes, I'm fine,' she replied standing up slowly. Bruno
helped her put her skis on again. 'Let's not bother with this
slope again. I don't want to kill myself just yet.'

'OK. We'll ski to the restaurant down there and have a
drink. Then we'll go on some nice gentle slopes. Follow
behind me.' Clare followed carefully behind Bruno.

'I've never liked ice,' said Clare. They were sitting at a
table outside the restaurant.

'Nobody does. But you get used to it,' replied Bruno.

Clare wasn't sure, but she thought that Bruno wasn't quite as open and friendly with her as he had been yesterday. He'd thanked her again for the previous evening and said what a good time he'd had, but somehow she felt he was more distant today. She hoped that what she was about to say was not going to cause a problem.

'I'd like to ski on that run that goes near the bottom of the Matterhorn. We did it yesterday, d'you remember?' asked Clare. 'I want to remind myself of where my grandfather died.'

'Fine,' said Bruno, 'but we'll have to go now. We have to go up on the cable car in order to get over to it. And that takes a bit of time.'

Clare waited to see if he would mention her grandfather. Then she realised that, like the rest of the village, he knew who she was.

'Did you know that the man they got out of the glacier this week was my grandfather?' asked Clare.

'Yes, of course.' He smiled at her. 'Everybody knows. It's not something that happens every day, you know. And you were identified as the granddaughter by the locals, probably from the minute you arrived.'

'Why didn't you say something to me?' she asked.

'Why should I? If you wanted to talk about it, you would. So I assumed you didn't want to . . . until now, that is.'

'If you're so clever, you can tell me what I'm going to ask next then,' said Clare, lightly.

'You're going to ask me if I know anything about your grandfather's accident, aren't you?'

'Yes. Do you?' she asked.

'Not very much,' he replied carefully.

'And do you know Ulrich Grunwalder?'

He nodded.

'Do you think you could arrange for me to talk to him? I really would like to find out what he remembers. I met him briefly a couple of days ago, and I got the feeling he recognised the name of Edward Crowe. But I didn't have time to ask him any details.' Clare crossed her fingers secretly, hoping that Bruno would agree.

'I don't know if he'll remember very much, he's a very old man now. But I can find out,' said Bruno standing up. 'Now, come on, let's get on the cable car – that is if you really want to ski the Matterhorn run.'

'Yes, I do, honestly,' said Clare with a smile. 'It wasn't just a way of introducing Edward Crowe into the conversation.'

About half an hour later they stood in the shadow of the Matterhorn. Bruno pointed out the hut which the climbers stayed in overnight before setting out to climb to the top of the mountain in the early mornings.

'You can walk up to there quite easily in the summer,' said Bruno. 'Look, there's the path. Can you see the rope at the side?' Bruno stood behind her and pointed.

'D'you think Grandpa Edward stayed in that hut in 1924?'

'Possibly,' replied Bruno. 'It was certainly there then.' Bruno looked up at the magnificent mountain.

'What are you thinking?' asked Clare.

'Just what a magical mountain it is. It must be one of the most photographed places in the world – you see it on every box of Swiss chocolates, and on every souvenir from Zermatt, but I never tire of looking at it.'

'How many times have you climbed it?' asked Clare.

'About twenty, twenty-five, I guess . . . to the top. And a few unsuccessful climbs too.' Bruno paused. 'It almost looks a friendly mountain in this light, doesn't it?'

'Mmmm,' replied Clare. He had put his arms around her from behind.

'It isn't. It can be a very cruel place sometimes. Come on,' he said suddenly. 'Let's go. It's getting late. We don't want to miss the last lift down to the village.'

*   *   *

The electric taxi stopped outside her hotel. She got out stiffly. Her left side felt painful as a result of the fall. Bruno leaned out of the window.

'I'll ring you later when I've talked to him,' he said.

Clare didn't need to ask who 'him' was. She was just pleased that he'd remembered without her having to ask him again.

'That'll be great,' she said. 'Thanks.'

She put her skis away in the ski room and took off her boots. What a wonderful moment that was! Ski boots were such big, unnatural things to wear on your feet. But it was almost worth it for the pleasure of taking them off at the end of the day.

In her room, she got undressed and was admiring some large purple bruises from her fall all down her left side when the phone rang.

'Hi, it's me,' said Bruno. 'Herr Grunwalder has agreed to meet you tomorrow. But I'd like to see you tonight. I need to tell you about something.' His voice sounded worried.

'What's wrong?' asked Clare.

'Nothing, well . . . I don't know. I'll see you later.'

Clare felt she was getting mixed messages from Bruno – one minute he was obviously attracted to her, the next he seemed to be putting a distance between them. What was going on? She didn't need this right now.

Chapter 16   *Bruno's story*

The long hot bath hadn't particularly helped Clare's bruised body. She was still moving very carefully when she walked into the Monte Rosa later that evening. Bruno was standing at the bar talking to some other men but broke away when she came in.

'I feel my age tonight,' said Clare after they'd sat down together.

'You don't look it,' replied Bruno smoothly. 'Your face is full of colour from being in the sun all day.'

'More like on fire,' laughed Clare touching her burning cheeks. 'Anyway, how did you get on with Herr Grunwalder? Was he really willing to talk to me?'

'He's agreed to – yes.'

'And did you explain who I am – I mean about being Edward Crowe's granddaughter?'

'He knew,' replied Bruno with a small smile. 'Like I said, everybody here knows who you are. All those men at the bar know who you are – and they're probably wondering why I'm talking to you, too.'

'What do you mean? Is there something wrong with me? Or is it because I'm a journalist and they don't want me to find out something? Or do they think it's ridiculous, this . . . relationship we're having?' Clare was beginning to get angry. She didn't like the idea that people were making judgements about her when they didn't even know her.

Bruno squeezed her arm gently. 'It's more to do with me than with you, really. That's what I wanted to talk to you about. First of all, I have to tell you that I'm Ulrich Grunwalder's grandson.'

'Ah ha . . . so that's how you were able to fix a meeting for me with him,' said Clare.

'Well, actually, I don't think my grandfather *should* talk to you, but I had to give him the opportunity if he wanted to.'

Bruno talked quietly to Clare. He told her that his grandfather had indeed been the climbing guide for Edward Crowe and Gordon Younger on their last expedition. He also said that throughout his life he'd always felt that there was something strange about this expedition. At first he'd thought that maybe his grandfather was to blame in some way for the deaths of the two English climbers, but nobody in the village seemed to believe this. And his grandfather had always said that it was a 'normal' accident – sad deaths, but it was a chance all climbers accepted. On the occasions when the name of Edward Crowe had been mentioned, either at home or in the village, there had been an uncomfortable silence, sometimes a look, sometimes a change of subject. Always something that had made Bruno curious.

'Obviously it hasn't been a major subject of conversation for years but it's always been there – in the background. Until this month, that is . . . with Mr Crowe's body reappearing.' Bruno paused. 'My grandfather has been very upset by the news. He's very disturbed and I don't like to see him like this. He's a very old man, he should be at peace at the end of his life, not troubled.' Clare was beginning to understand why Bruno had seemed confused in his relationship with her in the last few days.

'But he wants to talk to me,' repeated Clare.

'I don't know if "wants" is the right word, maybe "needs" or something else.' Bruno looked troubled. 'I don't know if I've done the right thing, telling him you wanted to meet him. Maybe I should have just left everything as it was.'

'It's his decision,' replied Clare. 'He doesn't have to tell me anything he doesn't want to, does he?'

'No, but . . . Once or twice in the last week he's tried to say things and then stopped. So I think he wants to talk about it.' Bruno looked directly at Clare. 'Maybe you are the right person for him to say it to. I hope so.'

'We'll see tomorrow,' said Clare. She and Bruno chatted for a little while longer about nothing in particular, but she could see that his mind was occupied somewhere else.

'I think I'll go back to the hotel for an early night, if you don't mind,' she said. 'See if a good night's sleep will get rid of this stiffness.'

Bruno walked with her to the front door of the hotel. He suggested picking her up at the hotel at eleven the following morning and taking her to see his grandfather.

'He lives in the family house. My parents live there too, but they will be out tomorrow morning, so it'll be easier.'

Bruno was obviously so anxious about the meeting that Clare felt quite motherly towards him. 'Don't worry. I'm sure it'll be OK tomorrow.' She gave him a quick hug. He kissed her hard and then walked off, leaving her standing outside the hotel door. Neither of them noticed Ulrich Grunwalder coming up the street.

Chapter 17   *Love story*

Zermatt, July 1924.

Ulrich watched as Edward bent down to kiss Marianne. He was shocked that they were so open about their feelings. And yet . . . Marianne, his much loved sister, looked so happy. Since Edward Crowe had arrived back in Zermatt at the beginning of the summer, Ulrich had seen Marianne open up, like a flower in the sun.

From the time he'd learnt about her feelings towards Edward, Ulrich had tried to get Marianne to see how impossible it all was. Edward was married, he was English, he was from another world and another class. He couldn't possibly love Marianne – she was fooling herself and would cause a scandal for their family and the village if she continued in this way. But Edward had told Marianne of his love for her and she believed him. Throughout that winter, Ulrich had been unable to persuade her to give up the idea of Edward coming back as a divorced man, ready to marry her.

'It's ridiculous, Marianne,' said Ulrich, many times. 'These things just don't happen. You are going to be very hurt.'

But Marianne had just smiled, and waited. Ulrich himself got married in February to Greta, a local girl, and left the business of talking sense into Marianne to their mother. At the beginning of May Edward returned, alone, to Zermatt. The relationship between the two of them grew. Ulrich was sure that people in the village knew what was going on, but nobody said anything to him. And he hadn't said anything yet to Edward, even though they had met several times. Edward never seemed embarrassed at seeing Ulrich – he even talked about climbing the Matterhorn together in a few weeks time. And Ulrich, despite everything, was excited at the possibility.

As the weeks passed, Marianne and Edward were seen together in public more – walking down the main street, occasionally taking tea in a small café. Ulrich learnt from his mother that Edward was not yet divorced, but, according to Marianne, it was only a matter of time. And now news of the affair started to reach his ears. He learnt that, not surprisingly, most of the people in the village didn't like his sister's behaviour. And the locals thought that Edward Crowe was embarrassing himself and an old Zermatt family.

His mother begged him to tell Edward to leave Zermatt. She knew that Marianne would be heartbroken, but this man would cause more trouble if he stayed.

'I will, Mama,' said Ulrich. 'Next week, when we climb on the Matterhorn. It will be easier to talk to him when we are alone.'

*   *   *

At eleven the next morning, Bruno and Clare entered Ulrich Grunwalder's house rather nervously, both wondering what was going to be said. Bruno had asked Clare to be patient.

'He's old, remember. His mind is still good, but he does wander off the subject sometimes. Don't hurry him. He'll get to the point eventually – if he wants to.' The old man was sitting at the table in the kitchen, looking straight ahead.

'Grandfather, this is Clare Newton. Do you remember?' said Bruno in what Clare assumed was a local language, a dialect, as it sounded very different from the German she knew.

'Yes,' he replied.

Clare shook his hand and sat down across the table from him. Neither of them mentioned the fact that they'd met a few days before.

'Does he want to talk in German?' she whispered to Bruno. 'I might need you to help if he does.'

'I will speak English. And Bruno, you will stay with us. Now Madame, what do you want to know?' Herr Grunwalder's voice sounded quite firm and clear.

'I would like to know how my grandfather died,' said Clare simply.

'He fell off the Matterhorn, and he pulled his friend with him. They both died. It was an accident, but there are always accidents in the mountains.' Ulrich Grunwalder stopped.

'The other man, Gordon Younger, was a friend of his, you say?'

'They certainly knew each other well. I remember they talked a lot together.'

'Where on the mountain did the accident happen?' asked Clare. 'Were you still on your way up, or coming down?'

'We had reached the top. We were all very delighted, especially Herr Crowe. Have you been up to the top, Madame? No, no, of course you haven't . . . It is magnificent. I have been to the top many times. The last time with Bruno.' Herr Grunwalder smiled at Bruno and held his hand. 'Now I am not able to any more. It is finished for me,' he said with a deep sigh.

Nothing was said around the table for a few minutes. Clare realised she would have to gently remind him.

'So you were on your way down then?'

No answer. Clare repeated the question.

'Yes, we were coming down. The Englishmen were tired, so we were going slowly. We were all roped together. We decided that only one man would move at a time, and that each man must secure the rope between each move. I was in front, then Edward Crowe and then Herr Younger.' Clare got the feeling that he had told this part of the story many times before. It was coming out very smoothly.

He continued. 'I moved forward, secured the rope and turned round to watch the next man. I was surprised to see that they were both standing together. Herr Younger had moved forward when it was not his turn. I started to shout something but just then . . .' Herr Grunwalder's hands started shaking. 'Just then, your grandfather lost his footing and he fell and . . . then Herr Younger fell too. He didn't have time to secure the rope, you see.'

'And you, Herr Grunwalder?' asked Clare. 'How did you manage to stop yourself falling too?'

'The rope. I had secured my rope. But it broke. The weight of the two bodies hanging. The rope broke and they fell to their deaths.' His voice was very quiet now. 'There was nothing I could do. They disappeared from my view.'

Clare could imagine the horror he must have felt at the time. He would have had to climb down with just his thoughts for company, and then face everyone in the village when he returned without his clients. He would have had to explain over and over again what had happened. Some people might even have believed that Herr Grunwalder had been responsible in some way. She was sure that his name as a good guide would have suffered – maybe not with the villagers but certainly with the foreign climbers who might have seen him as an unlucky guide.

'Gordon Younger is buried in the cemetery here,' said Clare. 'How was it possible that his body was recovered but not my grandfather's?'

Herr Grunwalder pulled a large handkerchief out of his jacket pocket and blew his nose. He slowly raised himself from his chair and with the help of Bruno walked out of the room.

'He'll be back soon,' said Bruno on his return. 'He just wanted to get out for a minute. It's upsetting for him to remember. Your grandfather and his friend were the only two climbers he lost in his whole career.'

'That's what I wanted to know, Bruno,' said Clare quickly. 'Did he have a problem guiding again? I mean, did climbers still trust him and want to hire him?'

'Well, he told me that he chose not to climb again for one year, not as a guide, not by himself . . . nothing. Then he started again, and became the best, by far the most popular and successful guide for about forty years. He's an amazing man. He's always been very special for me.'

Ulrich Grunwalder came back into the room.

'The next day,' he said, 'I went up with a group of men from the village to see if we could find the bodies. Herr Younger was on the glacier, the rope had caught round a rock and Herr Crowe was hanging down in a crevasse in the glacier. They tried to pull Herr Crowe up but the rope broke again and he fell. We carried the other one down to the village. They had fallen about a thousand metres.'

'Herr Grunwalder, did you know my grandfather – I mean apart from as a climber?' asked Clare. 'He had been in Zermatt a few times, and I believe that summer he was here for quite a while.' There was no answer from the old man so Clare decided she'd better be direct. 'My family have got two letters from him to my grandmother, written from Zermatt during that summer. They said very strong things – mainly that he was going to stay in Zermatt and never return to his family.'

Ulrich Grunwalder moved nervously in his chair and his handkerchief came out again.

'Is there something you are not telling me, Herr Grunwalder?' asked Clare quietly. 'Ever since I first arrived in Zermatt, I've had the feeling that there is some sort of secret about my grandfather's death. Nobody wanted to tell me that you were his guide, for example. Why not?'

'Madame, I will tell you why. I know it is time to speak. But it is a sad story for your family and for mine. It all happened so long ago and times have changed. It probably wouldn't be the same today – I don't know.' Herr Grunwalder leant forward and began, 'Your grandfather was in love with my sister, Marianne. He came back to Zermatt in 1924 to be with her.'

There was a noise from Bruno's direction. Clare looked at him and realised that this was news to him too. Herr Grunwalder continued. His voice was almost a whisper now.

'It was not good – he was a married man. He'd been here

with his wife and daughter, everybody knew them. Then he came back alone. It was a scandal. I don't know if you can understand that; but this was 1924, it was not like today. Marianne loved him and I believe he loved her, but . . . Marianne never forgot him.'

'Is she still alive?' asked Clare.

'No,' replied Bruno. 'She died about twenty years ago.' He turned to his grandfather. 'So that's why Aunt Marianne never married,' said Bruno. 'She was the only unmarried person I knew when I was a child. I thought she was very strange.'

'She was always good to you, Bruno,' said Herr Grunwalder sharply.

'So,' interrupted Clare, 'you went climbing with this man who had brought shame to your family and . . .'

'Do not continue, Madame. You think I killed him because of my sister. I did not. I liked him, even if I didn't like what he was doing. But it is true that some people in the village thought that his death was the best way out for everyone – except Marianne, of course.' There was a tear in the corner of his eye. 'Poor Marianne. She also thought I had killed him at first.'

'So what really happened up there?' asked Clare, impatient to get to the truth.

'There was someone else up there, remember, not just us two,' said Herr Grunwalder.

'Gordon Younger?' said Clare in amazement. 'Why should he want to kill my grandfather?'

'At first, your grandfather seemed happy that Herr Younger was with us. He introduced him to me as a climbing friend from his home town. But the first night, when we were in the climbing hut, they had a big argument.'

'What about?' asked Bruno. Clare jumped at the sound of his voice. She'd almost forgotten he was there.

'Your grandmother, Madame, had asked Herr Younger to come and persuade Edward Crowe to return home to her.'

'And if he refused, he was supposed to kill him?' said Clare. 'You mean, my grandmother hired someone to kill him – it sounds too much like a Hollywood film to be true!'

'No, I do not think she said this to him,' said Herr Grunwalder shaking his head. 'The story is not yet finished. It was clear that Herr Younger did not really want your grandfather to return. I remember Herr Crowe suddenly laughing, and then he said, "Good God, Gordon! *You're* in love with Agatha, aren't you?"'

'And who did grandmother love, I wonder – Edward or Gordon?' Clare said quietly.

Herr Grunwalder answered. 'I believe she loved your grandfather. Herr Younger said so. He was very sad.'

'So after all this high drama you still decided to climb the next day?' asked Clare.

'Yes, the next morning they both seemed calm, and they both wanted to go for the top,' continued Herr Grunwalder. 'We climbed quite quickly. There was not much conversation between us – Herr Younger, particularly, was in his own world. The only time he said anything was when we got to the top. On the way down, well . . . you know what happened.'

'You said before that when you turned round, you saw them standing together, which they shouldn't have been,' said Clare. 'Are you telling me that Gordon Younger deliberately climbed down to my grandfather to push him off the mountain – to kill him?'

'I don't know. Certainly there was some contact between them but I do not know if he really wanted to push him, or if he lost his balance and fell. Nobody will ever know for sure.'

No-one spoke for a moment, then Clare said, 'Well, it's an amazing story. A love story really, isn't it? With a tragic end.'

'It is a story that has lived in this house, with my family, for a long time,' said Bruno as he reached out to take his grandfather's hand. 'I know this village and its people – I can understand why it is easier for them not to remember the past – and not want you to bring it up again, Clare.'

'Yes, I can understand it too,' she said, hoping that they didn't think that for her it was just a love story. In fact, she found it all very moving – and disturbing. She wanted to go away and consider all this new family history.

'I have not told anybody before about Gordon Younger and what happened on the mountain,' said Herr Grunwalder. 'It was not important at the time. It is perhaps only important for you to know, Madame.' He looked very tired as he sat back in his chair.

'Thank you for telling me,' Clare said. 'Next week will be the final part of the story – when I go back to England with my grandfather's body. There will be no need to remember Edward Crowe or Gordon Younger or me any more. It will all be over.'

'Yes, I believe it will,' replied Herr Grunwalder, and he smiled at her.

Chapter 18   *Shared experiences*

Clare sat in her room with a strong gin and tonic, thinking about her family. There was Grandmother Agatha, so proud of her tragically killed young husband, never letting anyone suspect that he had left her for another woman; and her own mother who knew nothing of her parents' romantic lives. And then suddenly she started to cry. For about ten minutes she cried like a baby. She thought of all the sadness, and some of the happiness, that surrounded her grandfather. He had been brave to come to Zermatt to be with Marianne; surely it would have been easier just to carry on with his normal middle-class life at home. But then maybe he was the sort of person who couldn't live a lie, the sort of person who had to be true to his real self. Clare's crying increased. She couldn't help comparing herself with her grandfather. She hadn't been true to her real self, whatever that was, for ages. Her search for knowledge about her grandfather had in some way been a desperate search for her own identity. Well, she hadn't found it; she felt lost and she didn't like it.

Eventually she stopped crying. In the bathroom she washed her face and hoped she was washing away all the self-pity too.

She had to ring Andrew to tell him about Grandfather and Marianne.

At the end of Clare's explanation, Andrew said, 'One

thing I don't understand is why Grandma Agatha kept those two letters from Edward. She spent all her life denying the truth but those letters destroyed her story. Maybe she actually wanted people to find out after her death.'

'Maybe – who knows?' replied Clare. 'How do you feel about it all, Andrew?'

'Bit sad – so many damaged lives.'

'Nothing new about that,' said Clare bitterly. 'Anyway, do you think we should tell Mum?'

'Yes, I think we should. There've been so many secrets already about all this, I don't think we should have any more,' said Andrew. 'I wonder if the name Gordon Younger means anything to her, or if she has any memory of a Marianne and Ulrich.'

'She was only about three years old. She might remember horses in the street, but not people, surely.'

'You OK Clare?' asked Andrew. 'You sound tired.'

'Yeah, I'm fine – a bit sad, but OK. Anyway, look, I've made arrangements for Grandfather to be delivered to Coopers Funeral Home late on Monday. And you say you'll get a service or something organised for Wednesday, so . . .'

'I know what you're going to say now,' interrupted Andrew. 'You're going to say you won't be coming up with Grandfather on Monday because you have to go into your office. That's right, isn't it?'

'Yes, you know me too well,' replied Clare.

'Well, just remember what we talked about before – no wild stories, please. It's going to be difficult to keep it simple, but think of Mum reading it,' said Andrew firmly.

'Yes, yes, I'll remember,' said Clare quickly, not wanting to talk any more about that. She hadn't decided yet how she was going to write this story for Kevin. They said their goodbyes.

Clare spent the afternoon on her balcony with the laptop; she started to put down some ideas for her article. It was such a good story to tell; it had everything – love, jealousy, danger, secrets, death and two endings separated by seventy years.

She was still playing with her ideas when there was a knock at her door. It was Bruno.

'Come in,' she said. 'I'm glad to see you. How's your grandfather?'

'He's OK, a bit quiet, I suppose,' replied Bruno and he bent down to kiss her on the cheek. 'Gone out for his usual walk. It was an amazing story, wasn't it? I didn't know anything about Aunt Marianne and your grandfather, you know.'

'I realised that,' said Clare, handing him a beer.

'It must have been really hard for her. And I'm sure there were people in Zermatt who would not let her forget the scandal she had created. Poor Marianne.'

Clare closed the laptop; she didn't want Bruno to see what she'd been writing. 'Thank you for helping me. I hope it wasn't too painful for you to hear.'

'No, not really. I'm glad I know everything,' said Bruno. 'My only worry now is how much to tell my parents. Apparently, according to grandfather, they don't know about Marianne and Edward. I asked him after you left.'

'Ah ha, another thing between your family and mine,'

said Clare. 'My mother doesn't know anything about it either – my brother Andrew is going to tell her.'

'Yeah, it's strange the way our family stories keep running into each other – Marianne and Edward, and now you and me.' Bruno looked at her.

'Yeah, of all the ski instructors in all Zermatt I had to get you.' Clare laughed. 'That's lucky – unless of course . . .'

'OK, I admit it,' said Bruno. 'When I knew who it was who wanted private lessons, I was curious. I wanted to know what sort of person you were. I also wanted to know something about your family in the same way as you wanted to know about mine.'

'And was that the reason you suggested our evening drinks too – curiosity about my family?' Clare was not happy at the thought that she had been used.

'No, curiosity about you. I like you as you – not because of all this business,' said Bruno directly. 'But somehow the family connection makes our friendship feel even . . . better. No, not better, more right, more natural, more . . .'

'Better,' said Clare.

'OK, better then. Do you know what I mean?' asked Bruno.

'Yes, we have a lot in common,' agreed Clare, not sure where this conversation was leading.

'Look, tomorrow's your last day. Have you got anything on? Would you like to go for a walk out of Zermatt, away from all this grandfather business for a bit?'

'Yes, I'd love to get away from everything,' said Clare warmly.

'OK. I'll pick you up about ten tomorrow morning,' said

Bruno as he walked towards the door. 'By the way, you don't want to do anything tonight, do you?'

'Yes, but no. That is, I'd like to but I've got rather a lot to do,' said Clare, waving a hand in the direction of the laptop. Even though she enjoyed Bruno's company, she felt she needed her own space this evening.

After he'd gone, she lay on the bed intending to let her mind wander over the morning's events, but Bruno kept appearing. She began to wonder if there really was something between them, something that might continue after next week. Or was she just trying to fill an empty space in her life? Well, they obviously both found each other interesting and there was definitely a bit of sexual chemistry too. Maybe tomorrow would be a good day.

Chapter 19 *The summer place*

'Do you think Edward and Marianne ever came this way?' asked Clare as they walked along a path at the side of the valley.

'Quite possible,' replied Bruno. 'This leads up to the fields where our family used to live in the summer. And I know Aunt Marianne loved it up there.'

'Is that where we're going then?'

'Well, we'll go past it – but we're going further on, further into that valley.' Bruno pointed to somewhere in the distance.

Clare walked on with a steady rhythm. They were well away from Zermatt now and the air was very clean. It was a warm April morning, nature was enjoying the spring sunshine and Clare was in love – not with Bruno, but with the landscape. She wanted to breathe in all the beauty and keep it there. The contrast to London was too much for her to think about.

She'd worked late the night before on her article. She'd decided to write it more or less as it was – as a slice of her family history and as a reminder of how society used to be. She hadn't named Gordon Younger or the Grunwalder family – 'a local guide and a local girl' seemed enough – but her family were in the article. There was no way round that. She had written the whole story very simply, without unnecessary detail, and felt pleased with it. It was a powerful piece.

Now, with that behind her, she was able to enjoy the day. The path climbed steadily across land that until recently had been covered in snow. The flowers that had been waiting under the frozen ground for months were beginning to appear, and the birds had woken up to the fact that with the arrival of spring they had to get busy.

'It's a brilliant time of year,' said Bruno. 'Full of energy and new life. Makes you glad to be alive, doesn't it?' He stopped on the path and put his arms round her. She was lifted up and turned round.

'Stop . . .' she laughed. 'My head's going round . . .' He put her down. 'Nobody's done that to me since I was about eight,' she said breathlessly.

'No, well, it's not something I do every day.' Bruno was still holding her. 'I'm in a strange mood today. I don't know – a sort of weight has been lifted.'

'Your grandfather probably feels the same,' she said.

'Yes, I think he does. He looked peaceful this morning when I left.' He gave her a kiss on the nose and said, 'Come on, I'll show you the family's summer place.'

They left the path and climbed up the green hillside. Bruno took her hand and pulled her up the last bit. They stood with their backs to the wooden house looking down into the valley.

'I could live here,' said Clare. 'The view is incredible.'

'A bit far from the supermarket, but it is wonderful, isn't it?'

'Does it still belong to your family?' asked Clare.

'Yeah, but we don't use it very much,' replied Bruno. 'We come up here for picnics during the summer sometimes, that's about it now.'

'Let's not walk on any further,' said Clare. 'Can we just spend the rest of the day here? It's so perfect.'

So they did. They lay on the grass outside, sometimes talking, sometimes not. They got to know a lot more about each other's lives and each other's families. They shared divorce experiences and she could feel Bruno's sadness when he talked about his children. She discovered that he very rarely saw them – they had gone with their mother to Canada after the marriage broke up.

'I'm going to miss you next week,' he said.

She thought about saying something amusing – like how he would be grateful to get his normal life back without some Englishwoman bringing up old memories – but she didn't want to play games.

'Me too,' she said, and meant it.

When they kissed this time it was different. Clare loved the softness of his lips and the way he stopped to look at her. She loved the feelings that it produced in her.

'That was nice,' said Bruno touching her cheek.

'Certainly was,' she agreed.

Neither of them quite knew what to say next.

'How do you feel about long-distance relationships?' he asked.

'I don't know, I've never had one. Have you?' she replied.

'Not really. But I don't want tomorrow to be the end of us.'

'No, nor me.' They lay there holding hands. Clare said, 'I saw this film once when the man and the woman, who were both married to different people, met once a year for a weekend of love and then went back to their normal lives. I remember thinking how exciting that sounded.'

Bruno laughed and rolled over to look at her. 'Sounds wonderful, but I think I'd like it more than once a year!'

'Agreed, but we're not kids any more, we don't need a twenty-four-hours-a-day sort of relationship, do we?' said Clare.

'I wouldn't mind one twenty-four hours now,' said Bruno kissing her ear.

Clare was still not one hundred per cent sure about a new relationship. And to make love, knowing that she had to leave the following day was just not her way. She tried to explain this to Bruno and he accepted it without problem.

'Once I've got everything sorted out back home, we can see how we feel. Maybe you'd like to come over to London and stay with me?' suggested Clare. 'We can take it from there.'

'That sounds very sensible, Clare. Very adult,' said Bruno, laughing. Later, on the way back to Zermatt they chatted easily together but Clare could feel that the nearer they got to the village, the more the outside world began to take over.

Bruno could feel her silence. 'Difficult, isn't it? Your body's here but half your mind is somewhere else.' This man was getting good at reading her.

'Yes, sorry,' she said. 'And I've had such a perfect day, too.'

'If it makes it any easier, I think we should say goodbye when we get to your hotel,' replied Bruno. 'We could meet tonight but it couldn't be any better than it was today, and you need to think about London things.'

'Are you always this sensitive to other people's needs?' she asked with a suggestion of surprise in her voice.

'Probably not,' he said cheerfully, 'but I'm getting better, obviously.'

Back at the Zermatterhof, Bruno came up to her room with her. Neither of them wanted to say goodbye in a public place. When they got upstairs they did the easy things first; they gave each other their addresses and telephone numbers, and made promises to be in touch on Monday evening. Then they stood and looked at each other.

'I can't believe I've only just met you,' said Clare. 'I feel I know you so well.'

'I haven't told you everything, you know. Still some things to discover when I come to London. You were serious about that suggestion, weren't you?' said Bruno a little anxiously.

'Yes,' said Clare and then waited to see if there was a little voice in her head saying 'but . . .' Nothing happened. 'Yes,' she said again. 'I'd really like you to come.'

'Bye then . . . for now, special person.' They had a long, sexy kiss which could easily have made them forget their sensible decisions. 'Let's make that London visit sooner rather than later.'

'Yes, please,' she said.

She felt sad and happy as she closed the door behind him. She really did like him. He was going to come to London; there was something good to look forward to.

She made herself ring Kevin. He was keen to have her finished story as soon as possible.

'Send it to me now, babe, if you've written it,' said Kevin.

'There are still one or two bits I'm playing with. I'll

e-mail it in the morning before I leave, if you really can't wait. And listen, Kevin, I don't want you to change a bloody word of that article. It's my story and it's good.'

'Course I won't change anything, darlin',' said Kevin automatically. 'You know how I feel about your writing. You're the best.'

Yuk, thought Clare. He really is a horrible little man.

'I'm being serious, Kevin. Change anything and there'll be trouble.'

'I heard you the first time. No need to threaten me,' said Kevin coldly. 'Just send it, will you?'

Chapter 20 *The news breaks*

Clare left Zermatt early the next morning. At the train station, she couldn't help looking around to see if Bruno was there, but he wasn't.

As the train went slowly down the valley to Täsch, she looked at the Matterhorn for the last time. She felt close to tears as it disappeared from sight.

The journey home was quiet. Everything went smoothly and at Heathrow airport she watched as her grandfather's body was moved to the funeral car for the journey north. Kevin's photographer was there to catch it all on film. She was sorry that her grandfather was going to be buried in the Lake District beside Grandma Agatha; really he should have been buried in Zermatt, his real home. 'Grandma got her wish, after all,' she thought. 'He's coming back to her after all this time.'

When she got back to her house, she wandered around, touching various familiar things and trying to feel back at home. But she felt flat.

The phone rang, but it was only Andrew checking that everything had gone OK.

She made one or two other phone calls to friends and caught up with their news. Then she rang Bruno.

It was picked up at the other end almost immediately.

'That was quick,' laughed Clare. 'Were you sitting there waiting for it to ring?'

'No, I was just about to ring you.'

Clare was happy to hear his warm, friendly voice, but it was odd talking to him on the phone.

'It's more difficult talking on the phone,' Bruno said. 'I can't see you.'

Clare laughed. 'You've done it again! You've just said exactly what I was thinking! You're incredible!'

'Thank you.' They talked for a little longer without really saying very much, but it didn't matter. The unspoken bits were the most important – there was definitely a current of excitement on the line.

After Clare had put the phone down, she felt better. It was clear that Bruno was important to her, he wasn't just somebody who had been part of the magic of those few days in Zermatt. 'Thank God,' she thought. 'I'm too old for a holiday romance.'

She was woken the next morning by the sound of the newspaper being pushed through the letter-box. Seven o'clock. Time for a cup of tea and a read of the paper in bed. 'I'll wait until the rush hour is over before I head off up north,' she thought.

She picked up the copy of the *Daily News* and went into the kitchen. Immediately, she turned to her article on page five. The headline over a full-page article screamed:

WAS HE PUSHED OR DID HE FALL?

'Oh no!' she cried. That wasn't what she'd written. What the hell had Kevin done? She sat down and, with growing anger, read the whole article. Instead of her gentle story of tragic love, the article had become a murder mystery, with Grandma Agatha seen as the jealous rejected wife.

At first, Clare couldn't believe it. She'd told Kevin not to change anything, and even if he personally hadn't re-written it, he was still the editor, still the one in charge with the final say. He could have stopped it if he'd wanted. Then the doubts began. Had she known deep down that he would do something like this, and had she chosen to ignore those feelings? She'd written the article and although a lot of the words had been cut or changed, she was still the guilty one. She should never have let herself be pushed into writing it. The article, as it had come out, was just another example of how low the *Daily News* had sunk – and how low she'd sunk too.

She picked up the phone, pressed Kevin's numbers with hatred, and waited.

As soon as he answered, she said, 'You're a complete bastard, Kevin. I resign.' And put the phone down hard.

Clare walked around the house trying to work things out in her mind. She found a packet of cigarettes in the sitting room that someone must have left and without thinking, lit one. A couple of puffs and she put it out in disgust.

Should she ring Andrew or her mother and warn them about the article? No, perhaps better to explain it all face to face. Oh God, she could see the hurt look on her mother's face now.

The phone rang, but she ignored it. Probably Kevin with some smooth excuse. She switched off her mobile in case he tried that number, and went upstairs to have a shower. The hot water poured over her, but it didn't wash away the anger she felt towards Kevin, the newspaper and herself. She'd been a blind fool, trying to pretend that she still had control over her work. But her kind of journalism had gone, big business had taken over and she was glad she was out of it, glad not to be employed by those bastards any more!

The drive up to her mother's gave her some thinking time. She thought about her future and the need for her to get control again over her professional life, but most of all she thought about her family. The nearer she got to the Lake District, the more nervous she became about facing them.

She took a deep breath as she let herself into the house. Her mother and Andrew were watching TV.

'Oh Clare,' said her mother as soon as she saw her. 'How could you?' And her eyes filled with tears.

Clare sat down and put her arms round her mother. 'I'm sorry, Mum,' she said and found that she was crying, too.

Andrew sat there in cold silence.

'I've resigned from the paper,' Clare said. 'I know it's too late but anyway, that's what I've done.' Then she told them how she'd originally written the article.

'I told you to be careful with Kevin,' said Andrew. 'The whole thing is disgusting – my opinion of newspapers and the people who work for them was right. They've got no normal human feelings at all. I could go on, but what's the point?'

Clare knew what journalism could be like and she accepted that Andrew and her mother had every right to be angry and hurt. She was too.

Later that evening, when everybody had said what they needed to say, the three of them were able to talk a little about Edward Crowe's life and death. There were several questions that Clare would have liked to ask her mother about Grandma Agatha, but she thought it better not to. It could wait. By ten o'clock, they had exhausted themselves. No more anger about the article, no more questions, no more to talk about. They went to bed.

Chapter 21 *Burying Edward*

The service for Edward Crowe was simple and private. Secretly, Clare had been worried that the *Daily News* might have sent a reporter or photographer, but luckily only the three of them were there. They buried him in the family grave next to the wife he had left. It was not a particularly sad occasion as Edward had never been part of their lives, except as a memory.

As they left the cemetery, a woman approached them. Clare immediately thought, 'Reporter'.

'I'm from the *Lake District Gazette*. Could I just ask you a few questions about Albert Crowe?' said the woman.

'*Edward* Crowe,' said Andrew angrily. 'At least get your facts right.'

'Sorry,' said Clare at the same time. 'We're not answering any questions.'

The three of them got into Clare's car and she drove off quickly. 'Why can't they leave us alone?' asked her mother in a shaky voice.

'They will, Mum,' said Andrew. 'It'll be old news by tomorrow, don't you worry.'

'He's right, Mum,' said Clare. 'Just forget it.'

Before Andrew left to drive back to his own home, Clare managed to talk to him on his own for about ten minutes. She wanted to know whether he was still very angry with her. She hated the idea of losing her brother's friendship.

He was angry, but not really with her. He could see how shaken she was by what had happened.

'What'll you do now?' he asked. 'Do you want to come and stay with us until you've worked out your next move?'

'That's a lovely offer, Andrew, thanks,' she replied. 'But I need to go back to London. For a start, I've got an interview with Cherry Gaskell arranged for Friday – it's important, you know, my first job away from the *Daily News*.'

'Take care, Clare,' said Andrew anxiously. 'Don't sell yourself to the first person who wants to buy. Remember, you're a writer not a journalist.'

'You're right,' she said giving him a big kiss. 'Thanks for reminding me, my lovely, sensible brother.'

Clare decided to stay on overnight. Her mother obviously didn't want to be alone and Clare was happy to have the chance to repair their relationship.

After breakfast the next morning, Clare drove back to London. She planned to go straight to the office. She knew that Kevin would not be there at that time, and she wanted to collect some personal things from her desk. Then she'd come home, have a glass of wine and phone Bruno. She'd missed speaking to him over the last couple of days. Maybe they could fix a definite date for his visit. It didn't have to be next week but it would be lovely to fix it for a few weeks' time, then she'd have something to look forward to.

But she didn't have time to phone Bruno. He phoned her.

'You won't believe this Bruno, but I was just going to ring you,' she said, realising the current of excitement running through her.

'I'm reading your mind again,' Bruno joked. They laughed and all the anger she had been feeling about Kevin and the article began to disappear.

'I thought I might come and visit soon,' said Bruno, and then added, 'Is something wrong?' He could hear it in her voice.

'Oh,' said Clare, 'I'll tell you all about it when I see you.'

They made plans for Bruno to come over in two weeks, and after they had hung up, Clare felt that this relationship was also the start of a new direction for her. Or perhaps, she thought, it was just part of something that had started with her grandfather and which she was just continuing with Bruno.

It made her feel closer to that man who had fallen to his death seventy-four years ago. Her grandfather had had a very romantic idea of life, perhaps in some ways as dangerous and beautiful as The Matterhorn itself. But now that she had discovered that feeling herself, that romance and that beauty, she knew it would be difficult to turn back.